THE COLLEGE ENTREPRENEUR

How to leverage your university to build a business, escape the rat race and live life on your terms.

By Kyle Gray

Contents

PART 1

Why start a business in school?

Chapter 1

YOUR UNIVERSITY, YOUR BUSINESS AND YOU

There it was… The symbol of years of investment, hard work and experience: my Master's degree. It came in a large envelope, it was printed on thick, high quality paper, and was signed by people I didn't know with fancy ink. This was my permission slip for success.

Or was it?

I knew better than to trust a piece of paper to give me what I wanted. I had gone through the motions to earn this paper, but it was not what I was seeking. I had different priorities.

I graduated with something far more valuable than a diploma. It had nothing to do with grades. It was not something that could be given to me. It was something I made myself.

Today, almost three years after graduating, that piece of paper is sitting in the same envelope it came in.

I spent eight years at a large public university. I started as a confused and misguided freshman. And, along with my classmates, I jumped through all the hoops to earn a Bachelor's degree. I joined the ranks of hungry graduates hoping that this piece of paper would lead to a better life.

After a few rounds of applications and interviews, I was able to get a full-time job on campus as an advisor. The job was good: it was in my field of study, it had benefits and a decent salary.

It was at this job that I learned a great deal about how universities work behind the scenes. I found that many of my assumptions about how universities worked were totally wrong. I discovered many ways students could leverage the system to their advantage.

Though it was a good job in the classic sense, I found that only a small portion of what I was doing was fulfilling. I felt trapped behind my desk, working for a system that did not work for me. I wanted to do something that mattered. I wanted to do work that interested me, that made an impact, and that allowed me to live life on my terms.

I started again as a student, enrolling in a graduate program with the hopes of learning how to start my own business. But I was not going to wait until I graduated to start. It was time to take action. I took advantage of what I had learned as an advisor, using the university system as a resource. I built key skills, valuable relationships, and received guidance on how to start and grow my own business.

I graduated as one of the top students in my class, but I didn't need to rely on my grades or my degree to attract opportunities. I had a business that was a consistent source of income. I had a valuable skillset that was sought-after by many businesses and startups. I had developed a personal brand and was recognized as an entrepreneur and marketer.

Instead of hunting for a job, job offers came to me and I could negotiate or turn them down if they didn't meet my standards. Instead of compromising my values or my goals to earn a paycheck, my interests and values became the source of income.

After graduation, I continued to build my skills in marketing and helped grow a startup to a million dollar business. I taught at an innovative startup accelerator at my university, helping other students become entrepreneurs. Best of all, I now have a business I can run from anywhere; I do work that is challenging and interesting and I do it on my own schedule. None of this would have been possible if I had just focused on getting good grades and hoped my degree would pay off.

You don't need to spend eight years at your university to get the same results. This book highlights the important lessons I learned and gives you the key strategies to do it in a fraction of the time. It's possible for you too, but only if you're ready to do what it takes.

We live in strange times...

For nearly 100 years, getting a university education was an undoubtedly sound investment. Graduates were almost guaranteed brighter futures with steady jobs, comfortable salaries, and good benefits. While there are still many great advantages to a college education--some of which we will explore in this book--the decision to attend university has become more complicated in recent years.

The promises of a degree seem more and more tenuous with each year, especially as the cost of tuition rises while incomes remain stagnant. Many jobs that were once highly valued are being lost to technology and outsourcing, and this trend is likely to continue.

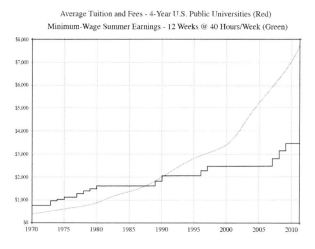

Average Tuition and Fees - 4-Year U.S. Public Universities (Red)
Minimum-Wage Summer Earnings - 12 Weeks @ 40 Hours/Week (Green)

Furthermore, many leading businesses and organizations are openly stating that a degree has little impact on an applicant's chances of being accepted.

"This week, international publishing house Penguin Random House decided to drop degrees as a requirement for job applicants, following in the footsteps of major consulting firms Ernst and Young and Price Waterhouse Coopers.

The move comes as smaller employers are shifting away from hiring graduates or university students, believing kids are coming out of university with "no real skills" or simply being taught the wrong things." - University degrees 'irrelevant' to big employers

The job market has shifted as well. With the rapid change brought by quickly advancing technology, people need to be ready to make fast transitions and adaptations to stay competitive in the modern job market.

"Ninety-one percent of Millennials (born between 1977-1997) expect to stay in a job for less than three years, according to the Future Workplace "Multiple Generations @ Work" survey of 1,189 employees and 150 managers. That means they would have 15 – 20 jobs over the course of their working lives!" - Job Hopping Is the 'New Normal' for Millennials.

It seems like universities have been slow to adapt to these changes. Universities are optimized to prepare graduates for long careers with only a few transitions between jobs. In the past, this model worked. It used to be that new graduates could count on job security. However, the recent recession proved that job security was an illusion. Both young and old lost their jobs and were unable to find new work.

Even tech giants that seem to be stable aren't safe. This report from April 2016 covers Intel, one of the world's biggest manufacturers of semiconductors, revealing a plan to cut a massive branch of it's workforce after poor earnings:

"Intel Corp. will eliminate 12,000 jobs, or 11 percent of its workforce, embarking on the deepest cutbacks in a decade to gird for a fifth year of declines in the personal-computer market." - Bloomberg - Intel to Cut 12,000 Jobs, Forecast Misses Amid PC Blight

The workforce has also changed. Where older generations were satisfied with security, young people seem more interested in finding meaning, inspiration and purpose.

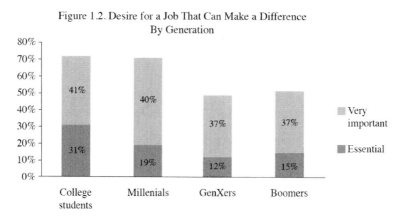

Figure 1.2. Desire for a Job That Can Make a Difference By Generation

Responses to: "Having a job where I can make an impact on causes or issues that are important to me"

"Most university students — 65 percent — expect to be able to make some positive social or environmental difference through their work..." - Net Impact Talent Report

This begs the question: is going to university still worth it?

Absolutely. I believe with a shift in your perspective and expectations, universities are still one of the best places to better yourself, and increase your opportunities. But if you're just focused on earning a degree, you'll miss the true value of the experience.

Imagine for a moment graduating with a source of income that can't be taken away by a boss. Instead of sending your resume to dozens of employers without receiving a response, jobs are being offered to you and you get to be the one who filters through them. Instead of taking a low-paying job that bores you and wastes your talent, you are doing work that you love and are abundantly rewarded for it. Instead of taking orders from an angry boss you are the one who makes decisions. You set your own schedule.

That's a great picture, right?

You might be thinking "Ok, I get it, it's a good time to start a business. But why while I am in school? I am busy enough as it is."

Starting a business is a process of self-discovery and self-development that can dramatically improve your experience at your university. Here are nine reasons why starting a business before you graduate could be the best thing you do for your academic career:

1. It's a chance to discover and follow your passion:

You need time to practice with different interests, skills and relationships to figure out what it really is you want. You don't have to wait until you graduate to do this. Starting a business will give you the chance to experiment with all of these things and test them in the real world.

Instead of just following the same script of "work hard, get good grades" and hoping for the best, a business will teach you what is truly valuable, and will reward you for it. Experimenting with your business while in university will help point you to the key skills that will make a difference in your business and your life.

2. You have advantages as a student that will disappear once you graduate

Students have certain resources and advantages both on and off campus that make starting a business and growing your network easier. People are open to students with a desire to learn and will be more likely to help you. You have resources to bring interesting people to your university to speak.

A university is also one of the easiest places to meet like-minds. Whatever you're passionate about, it's almost a certainty that there are many more students on campus who resonate with your passion. You can build teams, collaborate and experiment together.

3. Time is your most valuable resource

You'll never be younger than you are now, and you'll never have more time than you do today. Starting early while the risks are lower will allow you to build a foundation of skills and relationships that will pay off in the long run.

4. You will learn to become a leader

Leadership is hard to find and harder to teach. Leadership is not simply bossing others around and delegating tasks. Leadership is inspiring others to be better; it is being vulnerable and sharing your ideas and perspectives even when unpopular. It is being an example who others can look up to and model themselves after. Leadership is being able to see the best in others and to find ways to bring it out.

Starting a business forces you into a role where you are actively cultivating leadership with everything you do. Even if you do not have any other team members, you practice leadership with your customers and the people you interact with. You experiment with projects and whether you succeed or fail, you learn from the results. You take responsibility for helping a group of people, and take pride in the value you can add to their lives.

5. You will learn and adapt quickly

Starting a business will force you to take many risks and chances. Whether or not you fail or succeed in these risks is less important than your attitude towards them. Learning from whatever results you get and applying those learnings in a helpful way will lead to success.

Growing a business requires a broad set of skills; many of these skills are evolving and changing constantly. As you constantly challenge yourself to develop new skills, you will discover your own learning process and find ways to pick up new information quickly.

6. You will learn how to build trust and gain attention

As an entrepreneur, your competitive advantage will be the trust and attention you build and cultivate with your audience and customers. It will be the story you tell that inspires and engages people. As you learn what interests them and what their problems are, you'll be able to find more ways to help them and connect with the people around you. Learning to capture the attention of the people you want to help and build trust with them will be one of the most influential and powerful skills you will ever learn.

7. It is a source of freedom

I have seen too many brilliant graduates settle for uninspiring jobs after they graduate. They give up more than they realize. They trade away precious time, energy, and some of the most valuable years of their life to a job that makes them feel sick inside. Settling for that job closes the door to other opportunities, because they stop looking for them.

With a business up-and-running before you graduate, you won't need to settle for a job you dislike. If your business is providing you with a steady income, you may decide that working for someone else is not something you want. With the entrepreneurial skillset you develop while building your business you may never have to rely on others for a steady income ever again.

8. It leads to better job opportunities

If you decide you do want to work for someone else, having a business is one of the greatest resume builders out there. It proves you can take initiative, get results and solve problems.

Starting a business gives you something solid and tangible to show employers when you graduate. They will consider you for more competitive positions in leadership and management. This means better pay, more respect, and more interesting work.

On his blog post called "**No Direction Home**" Seth Godin discusses the key to success in job market:

"The thing is, whether you're a newly graduating senior (in hundreds of thousands of dollars of debt) or a middle-aged, experienced knowledge worker looking for a new job, what the best gigs want to know is:

- Can you show me a history of generous, talented, extraordinary side projects?
- Have you ever been so passionate about your work that you've gone in through the side door?
- Are you an expert at something that actually generates value?
- Have you connected with leaders in the field in moments when you weren't actually looking for a job?
- Does your reputation speak for itself?
- Where online can I see the trail of magic you regularly create?"

Your business can be all of the things that Seth listed above. It will make you interesting. It will be the source of your stellar recommendation letters; it will be hard evidence that you can get results. This will not only lead to more job opportunities, but high quality opportunities and a higher starting salary.

9. You'll build a powerful network

For better or worse, the common saying "it's not what you know, it's who you know" is very true, and much of your success in life will be based on building meaningful connections and relationships. Every big leap forward or big opportunity in my life has come with help from someone who has known and trusted me.

You want to start as soon as possible, because a good network takes time to build. You need to grow valuable relationships over a span of months and years. Starting early will help ensure that you have the connections and relationships developed that will be key in helping you land the next big opportunity.

Starting a business before you graduate will also build your network in places that most students don't get exposure. You'll start interacting with influencers in industry, local business owners in your city, and thought leaders around the world. These are the kind of connections that will lead to better results when you graduate.

How to use this book

Despite what some people may tell you, there is no blueprint for a successful business. Though there are many helpful guidelines, you'll have to discover your own path.

Treat this book like a playbook that you can flip through to find different useful strategies. Depending on where you are on your path, different sections of the book may be more relevant to you than others. I don't recommend trying to implement all of these ideas at the same time, but you can combine some of these strategies as they feel appropriate for you.

Part 1: Explains the benefits of starting a business as a student. If you have never considered starting a business before, start here.

Part 2: Will help you discover your talents and your interests in order to make a plan for starting your own business. If you know you want to start a business, but aren't sure how to get started, look here.

Part 3: Is full of strategies that you can use to hack your university's resources to help you start and grow your business. If you have an idea of what kind of business you want to start and want your university to help you, start here.

Part 4: Personally, this is where things get really exciting for me. This section discusses the strategies that lead to the biggest results in my life. These are tactics for making connections with customers, thought leaders, mentors and other entrepreneurs off campus. If you have your business idea and are ready to start connecting with people off campus and in your industry, check this section out.

Are you ready?

I say it's time to take control of your education, think differently, and create something amazing. Going through this process of discovery and creating a business will be a great adventure. It won't always be easy and you can't always be sure of what will happen next. But like any great adventure there are great rewards if you see it through. I can't guarantee you'll create the next billion-dollar startup, but I can guarantee you'll come away with a better understanding of yourself, with powerful relationships, and with valuable skills.

Let's get started!

Chapter 2

9 MYTHS ABOUT BUSINESS

Travel was an obsession of mine. I loved not simply traveling to a new city for a week to see the tourist attractions, but to live in different locations, learn the language and spend time in a different culture than my own. I had done this before by doing an exchange to a university in Argentina, but I still remember the cold realization that once I returned and graduated, this kind of life would not be available to me anymore. I was going to have to get a job, and would only have a few weeks off a year. Time for a quick vacation, but not to embed myself in another country. That was my reality: it's what my friends were expecting, it's what my family was expecting, it was what I saw on television; that was the path.

Eventually I discovered a different group of people living lifestyles that resonated with me. I came across podcasts and blogs with stories of entrepreneurs who claimed to be average everyday people, but who had businesses that would allow them to travel, build wealth and do work they were passionate about (or that would allow them the lifestyle to pursue their passions) at the same time. They called themselves location-independent entrepreneurs.

I had never considered the idea of being an entrepreneur. I never imagined myself to have what it took to start a business. It felt like a bad thing to want to start a business and turn a profit. I felt that businesses in their blind pursuit of profit were trying to extract value from the world without giving anything back. It was a myth I believed, but I didn't realize it.

These location-independent entrepreneurs were different: they were building businesses that helped people, that added value. They weren't greedily pursuing money, but were trying to create something great.

Still, I didn't think I could do it for myself. I had no idea how to start a business. I didn't have an amazing idea, I had never studied business, and I did not have technical skills like programming. So instead I spent years simply consuming these stories of other people, like a curious child looking through a hole in the fence, but never daring to climb it.

Myths--false stories I had learned without noticing and that I believed without questioning--held me back for years. The belief that I did not have what it took to start a business, that trying to profit from what you create is wrong, or that my destiny was to work a 9 to 5 were all incorrect. They kept me from even trying.

Eventually something changed. A small change, like a tiny pebble rolling down a mountain, but eventually grows into an avalanche that shakes the ground. I chose to take action, a small action, to try putting together something that could generate income.

The myths that hold you back

There are many myths around the idea of entrepreneurship. Some were true in the past, but aren't anymore. Others have never been true but are convincing nonetheless. But once you see them as myths, they lose their power. Take a look at these 9 myths, and see if any are holding you back.

1.Business is evil

There's an impression that "start a business" means "extract profits and value and give as little as possible back in return."

Though it's understandable to feel this way, it is very far from the whole truth, and it is not a helpful thought.

Starting a business is about solving a problem or adding value to people's lives. Whether it's by providing information, a service, or a product, you make your customers' lives easier and they are happy to pay in exchange for it.

2. Businesses need to make millions of dollars

Often the only stories we hear are about startups like Instagram (selling for billions of dollars) or like Uber (appearing out of nowhere, disrupting the way we see the world, and making billions from it). These stories are entertaining, but they are often unrealistic. Most entrepreneurs start in a small way and grow over time. They make enough to live a comfortable lifestyle, but never catch the eye of Tech Crunch or Forbes. It's perfectly fine to have a business like this. Find a way that you can make an impact for a small group of people, and build out from there.

3. Students don't have enough experience to start a business

Perhaps this was true in the past, but in the last 10 years technology like Skype, crowdfunding, Paypal, and social media have made it possible to start a business from your dorm room. More and more students are creating businesses that are innovative and successful.

Students like Chris Cantwell, who between working on his double science & engineering majors reinvented chess and created a board game called **Quantum Chess** that captured the imagination of scientists like Stephen Hawking. Or students like David Toledo who invented a camping pot that charges your phone with excess energy from the heat and built a company around it called **Power Practical**.

4. Only business students can start businesses

The truth is an art student (or a student from any other field of study) is just as capable as a business student of starting a business. Your field of study and your personal interests give you a unique perspective on the problems you want to solve or on the people you want to serve.

Many of the most valuable lessons essential to entrepreneurship can't be learned in a classroom, and thus aren't exclusive to any field of study. The key ingredients are simply interest in an idea, courage to take action, and to be able to learn quickly from your experience and iterate on it.

5. I can't teach myself to start a business

Many people think that before they are allowed to start a business they need to take a class or get some advice from a business guru. Though it is important to connect with thought leaders and influencers in areas related to your business, simply consuming content will not get you closer to starting a business.

The true secret to being an entrepreneur is to take action. You will be your own best teacher in this process. Instead of seeking out a business guru, find other students who have similar desires to start a business, and learn from each other. A community of people dedicated to achieving a goal can help each other learn much faster than a single teacher can. As you continue to learn and gain experience, you'll be able to do more than just consume content from thought leaders. You'll be able to share your ideas and experiences and start a conversation.

6. Starting a business is expensive

Currently the most powerful tools for business are completely affordable. Facebook, Instagram and Twitter give you access to billions of potential customers and spread the word about your business. All for free! Creating a blog on WordPress or Squarespace can cost less than $100 to get started and only a few dollars each month to keep running. But creating content that is interesting and helpful can bring you thousands of customers each month. Even creating a new product can be financed by customers before it's made. Many students have used crowdfunding to take an interesting idea and get early fans to pay for it and make it into a reality.

7. I need to be a computer genius to have a business online

It has never been easier to build a website that's both beautiful and functional. It seems like almost every week a new tool to make the process even easier comes out. Software like **WordPress**, **SquareSpace**, and **SquareHook** are easy to use. You can start for free and practice building sites, learning as you go.

There's also an unlimited amount of information out there to help you through any hang-up. A simple search in Google can pull up tutorials and videos to solve almost any setback, and there's online communities and forums with a wealth of information for any technical issue you may have.

8. A business takes a lot of time

Another common image that pops into people's heads when imagining starting a business is the overworked startup founder that's putting in an 80 hours work-week to build their startup.

Though this is a fact for some businesses, it does not have to be for yours.

You could easily build a business that you ramp up for one season or part of the year and then spin down. You can also keep a small business running with just a few hours of work each week.

There are many ways to hire out help at a very affordable rates (yes, even for college students) as well as automating many of the tedious and time consuming tasks that accumulate with growing a business.

9. I can't compete with other businesses in my space

It's important to realize that competition is a good thing. It is a sign of a healthy marketplace. Whether you're creating a service, information or a product, there is room for you to create a solution with something unique and special to you.

Doug and Jimmy from **Minaal** were just two guys from New Zealand who loved to travel. They wanted to create a better travel bag for people who worked online and were frequently moving to new locations.

Many people told them they were crazy. The luggage market is very competitive and there was no way to easily break into major retail locations where the major companies dominated sales. Plus they didn't have any experience making a bag before, or working with manufacturers.

Doug and Jimmy developed their bag over a year learning about marketing, manufacturing and fulfillment in the process and launched their product with a six-figure crowdfunding campaign on Kickstarter.

They didn't topple Samsonite, but they found a unique need in the market that the big players were not meeting. They made a better product and carved their own space in a cutthroat market dominated by large companies.

Key Takeaways

- Examine your beliefs about business; are any myths holding you back?
- A good business creates value and makes the world better, it does not exploit people for profits.
- A business does not need to take a lot of time, make a lot of money, or be valued at a billion dollars to be successful.
- You can start a business even if you're not a computer genius, business student or experienced entrepreneur.

Chapter 3

DON'T DO WHAT OTHERS WANT

I woke up screaming again...

I rubbed my eyes and looked around. As my mind cleared from the nightmare I felt a wave of embarrassment, and I looked across my dorm room to see if I had woken my roommate. Fortunately, he was gone, off in another student's room pulling an all-night bender on "World of Warcraft."

The doctor told me my nightmares were probably caused by stress. Weren't these supposed to be the best years of my life? What could I possibly be so stressed about?

It was my freshman year at the University of Utah. It seemed like my whole life up to this point had been preparation for college. Now that it was here I felt like I had been blindsided; I did not have a major declared, and I had no idea what I really wanted to do with my life or for a "career." I remember feeling absolutely panicked and hoped for some kind of singular answer that would instantly make my life's purpose clear.

My classmates seemed to have it all figured out. I felt guilty, like I was falling behind because everyone else seemed to have a direction and I didn't.

But slowly the hoard of pre-law and pre-med students began to break down.

While this didn't solve my problem, in a strange way it made me grateful for my uncertainty. I was not the only one who was unsure, and I was not going to let my path be chosen by someone else.

The price of compromise

The biggest mistake you can make in your university career is to go through your entire education doing what other people want. It can sometimes be hard to tell the difference between what we want and what is expected of us. Things like culture, advertising, experiences, and family all work to influence. We are so consistently exposed to these influences, that others' ideas become our own and we lose track of ourselves.

This leads to a downward spiral of unhappiness and an unhealthy lifestyle. Instead of pursuing your "dream job" you take the "safe bet". Your work becomes drudgery, tasks to grind though until the day is done just to earn a paycheck. Day after day piles up and amounts to nothing but poor health and unhappiness.

It's sad to imagine for one person, but now imagine it on the scale of millions of people. How many brilliant technologies have gone uninvited, works of art left uncreated, secrets gone undiscovered because of this compromise?

This is what Ken Robinson refers to as a "human resources crisis" in his TED Talk "Bring on the learning revolution":

"But I believe there is a second climate crisis, which is as severe, which has the same origins, and that we have to deal with with the same urgency.

But this is a crisis of, not natural resources -- though I believe that's true -- but a crisis of human resources.
I believe fundamentally, that we make very poor use of our talents. Very many people go through their whole lives having no real sense of what their talents may be, or if they have any to speak of."

Pressure from parents

Often this is from parents. They typically have strong opinions of how you should spend this precious time of yours.

They often encourage you to go on a "safe path". Which means a path similar to what they chose, or at least what they believe will lead to financial stability for you. They mean well. But they often won't understand your goals, or direction you are taking.

This behavior can be especially strong if your parents are immigrants. They probably worked incredibly hard to get to where they are, and their expectations and hopes for your future was fuel for the fire that got them here. It can be incredibly intimidating to go against those expectations if they don't line up with your goals or passions.

Even if they do understand or admire your goals they may still advise you to take a conservative path and save your dreams for later. Why would they do this? Parents don't want to hurt you, and they feel responsible for the advice they give you. If they told you to take a risk and you ended up failing, they would feel guilty for having encouraged you to do that.

By understanding the nature of your parent's advice, you can give yourself permission to disobey them. At first this will be difficult, but as you progress they may come around and support you.

It can be difficult to take a different path, but this is one of the most important decisions you will ever make.

Culture and society

There is a hidden script that society expects us to follow. You catch glimpses of it in movies, commercials, the news and from our peers.

You'll hear it in the questions people ask you. As you move closer to graduation you'll start to hear "what job are you going to get?" Once the job is secured you'll hear "When are you going to get a house?" Or "When are you going to get married?" You see this script unfold in commercials: the happy couple with a new house, the successful professional with a new car.

All of these questions assume that you have already made the choice to do all of these things, it's just a matter of when it will happen. It is a fine script to follow, but it is not your only option.

People tend to advocate and recruit for decisions they have made in their life. The people who are single will advise you to be single, the people who have kids will advise you to have kids. They do this because it helps them reinforce that they made the right decision in their own lives, not necessarily because it is the best move for you.

Going off the script can be scary, and can invite criticism. But it will also teach you about yourself, and allow you to create your own script, based on your own values.
What if I don't know what I want?

If you aren't sure what to do yet, that's ok, give yourself the space to discover it. Your time at your university is a time to discover your talents and to figure out how to put those talents to good use. This is a process of constant intro-spection and self-discovery. You'll learn though trying new things, making mistakes, and being willing to learn from them.

The good news (though it might not seem good at the moment) is that this is a process you'll work on your whole life. Though it's tempting to hope for a single answer to the question of "what to do with your life?," that simple solution is rarely the case.

In his post **"Screw finding your passion"** Mark Manson mentions how life is not about having answers, but about taking action.

"Life is all about not knowing, and then doing something anyway. All of life is like this. All of it. And it's not going to get any easier just because you found out you love your job cleaning septic tanks or you scored a dream gig writing indie movies."

The process of starting a business will help you discover your talents and passions in many ways.

Key Takeaways

- Sometimes it's hard to tell the difference between your desires, and other's expectations of you.
- Influence from parents is well-intended, but not always your best option.
- There are subtle cultural influencers that can influence your priorities and decisions, by understanding them, you take away their power.
- Doing something that interests you will and setting goals that are freely chosen will lead to an incredibly greater amount of success and happiness in your career.
- Only you have the power to make yourself happy and find a path that is your own. So make sure to always check yourself to make sure you are directing the course of your life and not anyone else.

PART 2

Discovering your business and telling your story

Chapter 4

WHAT ARE YOUR BASIC SKILLS?

I had just finished my undergrad degree. I had been rejected on a few job applications I put out. I was frustrated by my lack of success, but I didn't know how to translate my talents into job skills.

To get some help, I started attending a weekly event at the university career services center called "Job Club".

One week in particular an incredible speaker came to present to us. The speaker was a woman named Carla who helped improve performance by encouraging team members to better understand their personalities and their inherent strengths.

She gave us a DISC test, which analyzes your personality and then gives you some insight into how you work with others. The test also looked at what motivates you to work, and gave you suggestions on how to use those motivations to your advantage.

I had taken tests like this before, but never ones that related to my work.

I had never seen myself from this perspective before, I didn't know that my personality would lend itself to specific skillsets. Carla encouraged us to hone our strengths instead of focusing on fixing our weaknesses.

After her lecture Carla gave us the opportunity to talk to her about our assessments privately.

As soon as she mentioned this, I tried to subtly position myself near the door so I could be first in line to meet with her. This test was fascinating to me, and finally it seemed like someone was going to be able to help give me some of that "life direction" that I so desperately craved.

She pointed out that I was extroverted, and loved to learn. She pointed out that I was good at energizing and encouraging people, as well as taking in new knowledge and turning it into useful information to teach.

Though it was not an exact prescription of what I needed to do with my life, Carla showed me many strengths that I had used in the past (and would use in the future) to get good results in my work and my life. This helped give me some indication into what kind of work I should seek out.

How to figure out your basic skills

A good first step into discovering what you want from life and what kind of business you could create is by getting an understanding of your basic skills. Though everyone is unique, there are many patterns in our personalities that can be categorized and organized.

The most obvious of these categories is introverts and extroverts. Introverts charge up their energy by being alone, reading quietly, listening, and not being the center of attention. Extroverts are energized through interacting with others: going to parties, meeting new people, and talking.

People aren't completely introverted or extroverted; it's a spectrum and most of us fall somewhere in the middle. But by knowing if you lean to one extreme or the other, could make some inferences about professions and work environments that might be most comfortable for you.

There are many other spectrums of behavior that can help develop your understanding of your own skills. By developing an understanding of your own personality, you can build some guidelines as to what kind of work you enjoy doing, what motivates you, and where your natural strengths lie. Let's discuss a few ways you can discover your skills.

Reach out to those close to you and ask them about your "unique abilities."

It's often hard to get a clear idea idea of your personality or strengths simply through introspection. We all have biases and tend to overemphasize or ignore different aspects of ourselves. A good place to start is to gather some data from people you know and with whom you have interacted at various stages of your life. Pick 10 people. You might know them from high school, from your job, as old friends, or as mentors, etc. They need to know you well, and you need to trust them.

Once you have your list, send them an email asking about what they think your unique ability is. In your message, it's best to provide a little context. If you would like a template to use for sending these emails you can download one at Kylegray.io/resources/

Be sure to include your opinion of what you think their strengths and abilities are so you can give them an idea of what you are expecting them to write. This also ensures that you aren't just requesting their time without giving anything in return.

It's best not to send all these emails at once. It can be difficult to come up with a thoughtful email for each person. So make it a goal to send one each day for the next ten days and see what happens.

If you don't hear back in 2 or 3 days, send a little follow-up and give them a gentle reminder. If they still don't respond after that, then pick a new person to reach out to. You probably won't get responses from everyone.

Copy and paste all their answers into a single document. Highlight words that appear frequently and look for any trends. Even though you are reaching out to people from very different times in your life, you may be surprised how similar the answers are.

There's an additional way to get insights into your personality with this exercise. Collect all of the unique skills that you noticed about everyone you reached out to. You may also find similarities in the skills or traits you admire in others. Things you admire in others tend to be strengths that are within you as well.

Personality tests

There are countless personality tests available for free or cheap that can provide excellent insights into what your skills and talents are, as well as how you interact with others, and what motivates you. Below are three tests I recommend you take. They will each give you slightly different information, but they should also have similarities.

Tips for taking personality tests

Stay focused - When you are taking a test like this you should stay completely focused on the test. Don't have social media open in another window or a conversation happening at the same time. To get the best results you need to be fully immersed.

Complete the test all at once - Make sure you know how long each test takes to complete. Plan to finish the test all in one sitting. You should also block out time to reflect on the results of your test and connect the results with things you are experiencing in real life.

You could take this a step further by blocking out an afternoon and taking all of the tests below and comparing the results. You should see patterns form in the results. Some tests may miss the mark for you in some areas, but you should find some similarities between each.

How do the test results line up with the results you got from your unique ability emails?

Be honest and go with your gut - Some of the questions may be uncomfortable, or you may not like your answer to it. After a few of these tests you will start to see how they work and calculate. It can be tempting to influence the results by changing your answers. But cheating on this test and giving an answer that makes you feel better won't do you any favors.

For most of the questions you'll get an immediate gut-level answer, more often than not, that is the right one.

Born For This Quiz
The **Born For This Quiz** was created by author and entrepreneur Chris Guillebeau and asks questions that should help you understand the work environment and style that you will thrive in. The quiz was developed from much of the research that went into the book Born For This which goes into more detail on how to find the work you were born to do.

Strengthsfinder 2.0
StrengthsFinder 2.0 is an online test that evaluates your strengths based on elements of your personality. This also comes with a personalized guide and other materials with ideas for how you can develop your strengths further.

The DISC
The **DISC** test is a personality test that helps explain how you interact with others. Understanding how you relate to others can provide key insights into your natural talents.

Myers Briggs
Myers Briggs is a test that outlines who you are and why you do what you

do. At the end of the test you are given four letter that describe elements of your personality.

This test is almost like a horoscope, people share their Myers Briggs category like they do astrological signs. It helps give a basic impression of how a person see the world, how they interact with outers, and what motivates them.

Holland Occupational Themes

The **Holland Occupational Themes** tests your motivations and preferences within different career fields. This test will help determine an occupation that you would enjoy.

A piece in the puzzle

These tests should help give you a basic idea into what your skills are, but they won't have you the perfect prescription for how to live your life. The results are just one piece in a puzzle that you are solving. Take the tests with a grain of salt, and use them as a rough guide to help you determine where your true strengths lie and make a plan for how to best use them for your business and for your life.

Key Takeaways

- By understanding your personality, you can find some direction to what your natural talents are.
- Friends, family, and other people in your life may be able to see natural talents you did not notice about yourself. So ask them!
- Personality tests can give you insights into your skills, paying for a few tests is a good investment, but check with your Career Services center at your university to see if they have any for free.
- Make sure to be completely focused and honest when taking personality tests to get the best results.

Chapter 5

WHO DO YOU WANT TO BE?

Near my university's campus was a place called the "Zen Center", where I occasionally attended group meditations on the weekends t. Meditation seemed to be a good way to clear my head and relieve some of the anxiety I felt about not having much direction in my life.

One morning, I arrived and was greeted by a kind old lady and directed upstairs.

The meditation leader sat on a cushion on top of a slightly elevated platform in the back of the room. Everyone called him "Roshi". I was skeptical of the ceremonial sounding name, but I was new to this meditation thing and was willing to play along.

Roshi asked us to visualize a prison and then to describe what we saw and what it meant. The answers were diverse and creative. Some imagined the expectations of others as their prison. Others thought their own expectations and ambitions were theirs. They imagined thick walls, cold steel bars, and enclosed spaces.

Mine was different. I saw myself on a gray plane, a flat surface that stretched as far as I could see in every direction. Nothing was confining me, but I had nowhere to go.

There were many paths I could take, many promising futures that I could claim. I felt pulled in every direction but as a result, I was not moving at all. An eerie quote echoes through the open space of my prison.

"I saw my life branching out before me like the green fig tree... From the tip of every branch, like a fat purple fig, a wonderful future beckoned and winked... and beyond and above these figs were many more figs I couldn't quite make out.

*I saw myself sitting in the crotch of this fig tree, starving to death, just because I
couldn't make up my mind which of the figs I would choose. I wanted each and
every one of them, but choosing one meant losing all the rest, and, as I sat there,
unable to decide, the figs began to wrinkle and go black, and, one by one, they
plopped to the ground at my feet."* - Sylvia Plath, The Bell Jar

I was jolted back to reality by Roshi's next question. "We must let this suffering
go. What would a perfect world be like without this prison?"

I imagined an arrow appearing on the flat plane. Pointing straight toward
a goal, a meaning, a purpose. I followed the arrow and began to breathe
color into the flat gray world. The prison was gone, and I was on "the path."

Again Roshi's voice pierced my vision. "We can't live in a perfect world and
we must let this vision go as well. What would a world made up of both
suffering and perfection look like?"

I dove back into my imagination. Back to the gray plane. At first nothing
happened.
Then again I saw the arrow appear on the ground. It was not pointing in a
single direction but going out in a spiral. I began to follow the arrow again
and color flowed into the world. As I continued I saw family, friends, teachers,
heroes and other characters in my life both past and present.

It was then I realized the lesson that this "Roshi" character was trying to show
teach me. It was not about a single life direction or purpose. It was about
the journey itself and the people you meet along the way.

After this moment, I began to look at others in a different way. Instead of
trying to model my life from any of theirs, I could take the aspects I liked
about their lives, and use it to give me a rough direction to aim for.

In the previous chapter I mentioned that things that you admire about others often indicate strengths in yourself. Though every person's life situation is different, we can use the examples of those we admire to help guide us in our education, life, and business.

It's unlikely that any one person will be a perfect model for our lives, someone may have great achievements while struggling with a turbulent family life. To help get an idea of what is important to us we can look at people through different lenses and piece together the following different elements to find a good fit for ourselves.

Achievements - What has someone done or achieved that you admire or would like to do in your own life? These could be athletic, academic, personal or world-changing achievements.

Lifestyle - How do they live their lives? How much do they earn, where do they live? Do they travel a lot? Do they have a family they love? Do they have power and influence?

Philosophy - This "life philosophy" does not necessarily have to be the dry and confusing textbook philosophies. It is how someone sees their place in the world. It can come from religion, life experiences, spirituality, or hardships. Who is someone with a world philosophy that you admire? What is their purpose in life?

Work - Doing work that you love does not feel like work. There are many reasons why someone would love the work they do. Ideally it would facilitate all of the other categories mentioned above. Who do you know of that is doing work like this? What does their day-to-day look like?

If you are interested in a book that breaks down the day-to-day lives of many of the greatest minds in history, check out **Daily Rituals: How Artists Work** by Mason Currey.

All in good time...

It's probably easy to come up with people who are extremely successful, wealthy or brilliant. These people are often highly visible in the media and in stories. But it is often uncomfortable to compare yourself to them. Wanting to be the next Michael Jordan on the first day you pick up a basketball is only going to frustrate you.

So it is also important to use different time frames as a lens to help you determine what you want. Asking yourself who you want to be like in one year sets a different standard than who you would want to be like in ten.

One year
For one year into the future, think about people you know personally that set an example. They're not too different from you, and they are easier to relate to and understand how they achieved what they achieved. If we keep with the basketball example, it would be easier to aim to be like your neighbor who's a good dribbler and never gets the ball stolen from him. A year is a good timeframe to build or break a habit, learn the basics of a skill.

Five years
In five years you will probably have graduated, and will have a few years of experience developing skills. These people are still probably friends or personal connections and are still easy to relate to. Five years is enough time to completely change the trajectory of your life, establish yourself as an authority in a skill or area.

Ten years

Ten years is more than enough time to accomplish very big things if you are focused. Ten years is enough time to master a skill and become one of the best in the world at it. You may not know anyone like this personally so it is ok to use famous people or even fictional characters as an example here.

Twenty years

Twenty years is enough time to build a legacy. Put people who you admire that have changed the world in this column. Accomplishments of people in this column could be new inventions, scientific discoveries, political movements, and rare achievements.

It may be hard to tell for some of these, especially if you have never considered them before. The purpose of this framework is not to plan out your whole life, or to predict it. The goal is to get you started on thinking about what you want in the long run and what is important to you.

Having people, you admire as a reference is makes it much easier to relate to your goals.

I have created a simple worksheet to help you through this. You can download a free worksheet to help you at **Kylegray.io/resources**

The four categories I mentioned above are in in the columns, there are also four rows representing 1,5,10 and 20 years into the future.

Simply fill in each box with a name and a brief statement of what they have or represent that you want. Some of the boxes will be very easy to fill out, others may take some time to figure out. I recommend taking a few hours of undistracted time to sit and think through each column.

Visualize your goals

Let's face it's a spreadsheet with a few names is hardly inspirational. To transform it into something more interesting, I recommend creating a vision board. A vision board is a tool to help you focus on your goals. It is a mosaic of inspirational images that resonate specifically with you.

Personally, I like having a physical vision board. I use a small corkboard and pin my inspirational images to it. I'll hang it up in my bedroom in a place where I can see it easily.

Take your spreadsheet and find images that represent each of the traits of the people you listed. It does not have to be a picture of them, just an image that symbolizes what you admire about that person. Print out each of the images and pin them around the board.

Keep it in a place that is highly visible, and take time to look at it and imagine yourself with those qualities and achievements. Seeing it every day will serve as an inspiration and a reminder to you of what your goals are and what you want to achieve. Focus on growing that desire and that anticipation and use it to inspire you. You can update your board with new images as you learn more about yourself or as your goals change.

Key Takeaways

- Your admiration is a powerful tool you can use to direct your own life, you can get insights into your own strengths and passions by examining what you admire in others.
- Make sure to examine different elements of people's lives, they may have one quality that you admire, but another that you don't want for yourself.
- Use different time frames to help tell the difference between short-term, long-term and lifetime goals that you want to achieve.
- Connect your goals with visuals on a vision board and put your vision board in a highly visible place so you can see it everyday.

Chapter 6

HOW AND WHY TO START A JOURNAL

I have only been robbed a few times in my life. I don't recommend it.

One such time was in Brazil.

I was with my friend Mack in Florianopolis. We had rented a car and were exploring the island. We found many beautiful beaches, exotic fruits, beautiful women and colorful buildings. It was our last day; Mack kept talking about this "secret" beach at the south of the island, and we decided to check it out as our last stop before we left.

After leaving our hotel, we parked near the trailhead to hike over a hill to get to this beach. We didn't want to carry our belongings, so we put them in the trunk of the car and did our best to hide anything that appeared valuable.

And so we set out. The trail was muddy and slow. It took us about 40 minutes to arrive at the beach. When we arrived it was a truly incredible place. It was almost entirely empty, blue waves curled and crashed on shore. The sand was fine and white, it made a strange little squeak when you put your foot in it, almost like rubbing two balloons together. We hiked out to some rocks and watched the waves crash against them.

A few hours later we returned to our car. My stomach dropped as I went to open my door and found it unlocked. Before leaving the car, I had triple checked that I had locked it. I looked in the car and it appeared like nothing from the front had been stolen. Then I heard Mack's cry of agony as he opened the back to find our backpacks gone.

We both lost a lot of valuables. Passports, cameras, clothing and so on. Looking back, they were just things. There was only one item I lost that could not be replaced. It's the one thing I still miss to this day.

It was my journal. In this journal I had documented many years of thoughts, worries, lessons and revelations. It was a tool to capture fleeting moments, and make sense of the complicated predicaments I would find myself in. I loved to look back through the old pages and feel old thoughts and emotions. I would always marvel at how my thoughts had changed over time; the big problems of the past that once felt like hurricanes would seem like only a breeze in retrospect.

Our designed lifestyles

Students often are faced with one challenge in particular when starting a business, most without even realizing it. From a very young age we are conditioned to follow a schedule that someone else has designed for us. Most of our days as a child were organized and prioritized by someone else.

Because it is easy to follow a schedule that other people have set, it's uncommon for students to plan out ways to invest free time. The precious unscheduled time students do have is often squandered on video games, social media, or other unproductive activities. This causes days to pass by without any progress on goals, leaving students without much say in the direction of their lives.

Directionless business

Entrepreneurs face almost the opposite problem: there is no prescribed schedule or blueprint that they can follow to be successful. To succeed as an entrepreneur, you need to face your fears on a daily basis and constantly be pushing your limits to move forward. You aren't always sure you're doing the right thing, but you do your best to carefully plan and to spend your time on the most valuable activities that will pay off in the long run.

This pressure often leaves me with a conflicted feeling in my stomach in the face of this uncertainty. I am a big self-critic so I often feel frustrated that even after the progress I have made I continue to feel uncertain and unsure. Questions creep into my mind like: "Should I keep working today?" "Am I lazy?" "Did I focus on the most important activity today?"

I have found that I am not alone in this struggle. It is a common theme among most entrepreneurs whether they are seasoned veterans or new.

The solution to both problems - a journal

A journal can be a tool to help you solve both of these problems. Use it to plan out your days and weeks, to help you make small but measureable progress on your business and goals. A journal can help you develop the focus and the critical thinking you need in order to invest your time wisely each day. And it can help you develop a sense of happiness and control in your life: a mindset that is critical to your success as an entrepreneur.

An important part of building a business or achieving any goal is tracking your progress. You can do that by starting a journal. People have a tendency to overestimate what they can do in a day and underestimate what is possible to achieve in a year or more. Having a journal and a strategy for the journal is a way to ensure you make small progress toward your goals every day. Making small progress each day on your goals will quickly lead to progress and growth you did not imagine possible.

The five minute journal

A very easy way to start journaling is the 5 minute journal approach. It's an easy way to create some momentum from positive thinking early in your day and to help you focus on what's really important.

Start each day with this journal and write down a few basic things:

First thing in the morning

- What are 3-5 things that you can do today to make the day great? I call this, the "power list."
- List 3 things you are grateful for.
- List 1 thing you are great at or a positive trait about yourself.

Last thing at night

- Jot down 3 things great things that happened today.
- Describe 1 thing that you could have done to make the day better.

There's a journal designed specifically for this called the Five Minute Journal, but a simple notebook or blank journal will work just as well.

More about the "power list"

Making a short list of 3-5 things that I want to do or achieve each day helps me to feel accomplished every day. Give it a try! The tasks don't all have to be related to your business-- they can be about fitness, relationships, or any other aspect of your life that you want to improve. They cannot be obvious things that you are obliged to do anyway like "show up for work today" or "pay my credit card bill."

I review my "power list" at the end of each day and check off the tasks I completed. Over time, every day becomes a testimony to the fact that you have control over your life. This seems subtle, but having this sense of control can dramatically impact the direction of your life. You will become more confident. Goals that once seemed out of reach will become feasible, and you'll feel more sure of yourself.

Here are a few tips for creating power lists:
- Don't feel bad if you don't complete all the steps: If you did not finish each item on the list, don't beat yourself up. Learn from why you did not achieve it all today and make a list that is more achievable tomorrow.
- Start small: Build the practice be starting with small tasks that you can achieve and feel good about. You want to build the habit over time.
- Be specific: Make each task on the list measureable. It should be easy to determine when the task is finished.

Every few months review your journal. Take time to reflect and notice how you have changed. What were some big problems you faced a few months ago? Do they seem so big now? What were you afraid of?

Your daily habit of keeping a journal will help you stay focused and happy as you begin to build your business and achieve your dreams.

Gratitude in the morning

Writing out a few things you are grateful for each morning will help you start your day in a good mood and will put you in the right state of mind to tackle your power list. Gratitude is one of the most empowering human emotions; it energizes you to achieve more and at the same time helps you be happy with where you are currently.

Here are some tips on how to write your gratitude section:
- **Feel it**: For each item you write, take a moment to try and experience your gratitude. You want to feel it and experience it viscerally, not just list it and forget about it.
- **Try to keep it fresh**: Try to always write new things that you are grateful for, or at least new reasons why you are grateful for them.
- **Write small things**: Don't always write about big obvious things like "I

am grateful for my mom." Simple things like "I am grateful for that cloud that gave me a little bit of shade yesterday" will keep your list fresh every day, and teach you to be grateful for almost anything.

- **Put a positive spin on something negative**: Try to be grateful for something negative that happened that had a silver lining. Maybe you learned a lesson from a bad experience, or realized how important a certain friend was when he/she helped you through a challenge.

Brain dump

I don't do a brain dump every day, but there are certain times when this type of writing is very useful. I typically brain dump into a journal whenever I am experiencing strong emotions. This is usually just writing out the situation as if i were explaining it to a friend. Putting the emotions, I am feeling into words tends to resolve most of the tension I feel and helps clear my mind.

But the real value of brain dump journaling is being able to come back to the entry after some time has passed. Almost every time I read an old entry about a struggle, I have a new perspective and realize that the problem I was facing was not really a big deal, and I should not have taken it so seriously.

After reading through many of my past brain dumps, I also notice that tasks that once seemed challenging and stressful to me are mastered. Even though I still feel the uncertainty I have always felt, it is because I am continuing to challenge myself with new things. This turns the discomfort I feel into a sign of progress. This fact helps me feel better with the problems I face today; I trust that in time these challenges will be overcome like all the others in the past.
Take things slow

Trying to implement this entire journaling process from the first day may feel difficult and time-consuming. The purpose of all of these exercises is to make you feel good; if you end up being overwhelmed by journaling, you won't be able to build the habit and experience the-long term benefits. I suggest starting with the piece of this journal process that resonated with you the most and begin to build a daily habit around that one piece. Once you have it established that habit, will be easier to add the other exercises mentioned.

Key Takeaways

- A journal can help you make the best use of your time and to take small steps every day to tackle your goals.
- Write down a "power list" of 3-5 things you can do every day to achieve your goals. It will give you a sense of control and accomplishment.
- Starting the day by focusing on what you are grateful for will make you happier and motivate you to achieve more.
- It's healthy to dump your thoughts into your journal when you are stressed. It helps you process the emotions and gives you perspective.
- Start small with your journaling habit. Write a little less than you want to write, this will help you keep up motivation.

Chapter 7

THE BASICS OF A PERSONAL BRAND

In high school Vincent Nguyen was known for helping people with problems. They would come to him for advice on their life or how they could improve themselves.

He recognized this pattern early and wanted to leverage it to help people on a bigger scale. He started a website called Self Stairway, a blog on self-improvement.

Vincent didn't know where this blog was going to take him and he did not know what he wanted to do for a career. He trusted that if he could create something interesting and build an audience, it would help open doors for him in the future, whatever those may be.

He developed **Self Stairway** over time, posting weekly articles with helpful tips, and soon had a large body of work displayed. But things did not stop there. Vincent worked to develop relationships with others in the self-improvement space. He commented on others' blogs, started conversations, linked to other articles in his content and slowly strengthened ties with thought-leaders.

Eventually, an opportunity appeared. He saw a job opening for an apprenticeship with the **Empire Flippers**, a company that helped people buy and sell websites. They were looking for someone to help them market their service. The new hire would move out to the Philippines to work side-by-side with the founders, and eventually have the freedom to work from anywhere.

This would be an incredibly competitive application, and Vincent knew he was up against people with more experience than he had. He needed to find a unique way to stand out.

He reached out to Justin Cooke, the founder through his Self Stairway twitter account and let him know that he was applying and excited for the opportunity. His twitter account demonstrated that he had built an audience, and it linked to his website which displayed both the quality and depth of his work. He did not let his website do all the talking though. Vincent cashed in on all the relationships he developed while growing his personal brand and created a video montage of successful entrepreneurs all encouraging the Empire Flippers to hire Vincent.

By the time Vincent had gotten to the video interview phase, the founders were just hoping he didn't make large blunders or display any "red flags" so they could hire him.

Vincent spent a year working with the Empire Flippers, learning hands-on skills about how to grow a business. He developed marketing strategies, generated leads, connected with influencers, went to conferences, and continued to build his personal brand and reputation.

After that year Vincent launched his own business, **Growth Ninja**. He took the experience he had generating leads with Facebook Ads for the Empire Flippers and offered it as a marketing service.

Once again, his personal brand and the connections that his brand enabled him to build helped him acquire early customers for his business. A few of the influencers he reached out to for that video became friends of his and referred him to some of his best customers.

Vincent could have never predicted what would come from growing Self Stairway and investing in a personal brand. His careful and consistent work in creating a high-quality blog and developing relationships became a platform that he used to completely transform his life.

What is a personal brand?

Imagine a friend of yours is having a conversation with someone. Somewhere in the talk they get to a topic where your friend's eyes light up and they say "I know just the person you need to talk to about this" and of course, they are talking about you.

What triggers people to think of you? What traits and qualities are you known for? Developing a personal brand is the process of increasing the number of people who recognize these traits in you and deepening the connection they feel with you and with that trait.

You grow your personal brand through the actions you take, through publicly sharing your thoughts and taking a stance, through developing your interests and knowledge, and through growing relationships with people and organizations.

Why would you want a personal brand?

As you start to build out your personal brand around a certain trait or idea, people will begin to recognize you in association with that trait. They will come to you for help in the area, share their ideas and thoughts with you, and will send opportunities your way. This starts to have a snowball effect over time; more and higher-quality opportunities will start to come to you.

These opportunities will often be related to the core theme of your personal brand, but they don't always have to be. A well-developed personal brand will outshine any resume. Showing that you can capture attention for a personal interest of yours requires the same skills that many businesses are looking for in capturing the attention of their customers. This could lead to new and interesting work opportunities on other projects that you are excited and passionate about.

Growing your personal brand teaches you how to capture two of the scarcest and valuable resources of our time: the attention and imagination of others. This skill, if developed, can serve you in many ways in the future and can allow you to do work that you are passionate about.

If you have a blog focused on your personal brand and your thoughts, it leaves what Seth Godin calls a "trail of magic" and proves that you have the courage to take a stance on something and share who you are.

How to start building your personal brand

A personal brand not something that you can develop overnight, nor is it something that will ever be "finished." You take small steps every day that will add up to something very powerful over time.

Start thinking of yourself as a brand

A personal brand is about how you tell your story and how you show your true self to the world. Start considering the story you want to tell and how you will tell it. What do you want people to think of when they hear your name?

- Do you want to be recognized as an expert?
- Or for personal traits?
- Is there an issue that you have a unique perspective on?
- How can you help the world?

You personal brand can evolve and change over time, but you need to "plant a flag" somewhere and start.

What comes up when you google your name?

Though at first your personal brand will be more defined offline through the people you know personally, you'll want to be aware of what people will find when they search your name online.

If you have a common name, there will likely be someone else who shows up in the search results. When I first searched for "Kyle Gray" someone known as the "Angel Whisperer" showed up. If that's the case you have three options:

1. Overtake this person's ranking in the search by producing more content and building a bigger brand.
2. Differentiate yourself by a topic so people will find you when they search something like "Kyle Gray content marketing."
3. Differentiate yourself by using your middle initial or middle name online "Kyle C. Gray."

Get a simple website up

To begin staking your claim for your personal brand online you need to set up a simple website.

If you are new to building websites, I recommend going with a free version of one of the common tools. Here are a few of my favorites:

Wordpress: This is the most common website tool online, it's endlessly customizable and very powerful.

Squarespace: Easy to use and has lots of templates to make your site look great without having to be a designer.

Squarehook: A drag and drop website builder that has lots of powerful options for building an online store. Perfect for the crafty types.

For a personal brand, I recommend using your name as the domain. With the free option on any of these tools your domain will appear like kylegray. wordpress.com. Eventually you'll want to upgrade, but for the moment it's better to keep things simple and free. Using your name instead of focusing on a concept will allow your brand to evolve with you.

You'll want to create a few pages on your site that introduce you and what you are about.

- **Homepage** - Have a good looking picture of you and a tagline that sums up the personal brand you are creating in a few words.
- **About page** - This is where you can tell your story a little more. Write a few paragraphs about who you are, what you are interested in, and how you can help people.
- **Contact page** - Give people a way to get in touch with you. Don't share your email, but leave a contact form that connects to your email address, you can also link to some of your social media accounts that you want public.
- **Portfolio** - If you are an artist or a creative, share some of your best work.
- **Blog** - You'll start to post your thoughts and ideas here.

Start a blog

Your blog will be your main tool to start positioning yourself as an expert in the topics related to your business and toy our passions. Your blog will be a platform to help you leverage and grow your network. As you begin to interact with potential customers, mentors, and other influencers, you will want to document your experiences, learnings and revelations on your blog.

Though many people assume blogs are text-based, there are many other mediums you can use, each with their own advantages.

- **Text** - Simple writing is easy to produce, to perfect and to maintain. It is the most consumed form of content. Text is also the best for getting noticed in search engines. A good example of this is **Danny Coleman**, who writes about how to keep a healthy mind, body, spirit, and heart.
- **Video** - This can be as simple as talking into your smartphone or laptop, but can be more elaborate. Video is great because it captures the full attention of viewers and lets people see you, which helps to build a personal connection.
- **Audio** - Podcasts are one of the fastest growing types of media online. Talking about your own story or interviewing others is a powerful way to build a blog. Julien Marchand runs a podcast as part of his PhD research on student entrepreneurs called the **StudentPreneur Podcast**. The podcast is a passion project, but it connects him with many interesting student entrepreneurs, thus helping his research as well as raising awareness about the possibilities for students who are interested in starting businesses.
- **Images and graphics** - A picture can say a thousand words. Creating simple images that are entertaining or educational is a great way for visually artistic people to build a blog. A great example of this is **Brian Becker**'s personal brand site, where he has been documenting a challenge to make a new design every day for 132 days.

Maintaining a blog will ensure that you always stay a student in your areas of interest. This is a good thing. You'll always be seeking out new things to learn and share. Keeping your blog up-to-date will make sure you stay sharp and relevant.

You can download a marketing strategy template for your blog at kylegray. io/resources.

Tell your story

You are the core of your personal brand; the story you tell is what will ulti-
mately attract attention and build connections. Focus on what makes you
different from what is out there already. Use your unique talents and perspectives to set yourself apart.

The story you tell needs to be authentic and relatable. This comes primarily
from honesty and vulnerability. There are already plenty of people pretending
to be perfect online. People are looking for someone real.

When I talk about your "story" I don't mean writing out your day-to-day like
you would in a journal. You need to pick a theme that interests you or a skill
you are developing:

- Create content that shares lessons you've learned that others can use
  in their own lives.
- Talk about struggles you have overcome and how someone else could
  overcome them too.
- Talk about the process of building your skill and the ups and downs
  involved with that process.
- Discuss a social movement you are involved with, why it is important
  and what you are doing to advance it.
- Inspire others to make their day a little bit better, and talk about challenges you have overcome.
- Do something that will make people smile.

Don't sugar-coat things; talk like yourself and be yourself. People will see
through any act you put on and will disconnect with you. This means sharing
stories about your failures as well as your strengths.

This will mean sharing the thought that you are nervous to share. Or taking a stance that is unpopular. Though these things will be the most difficult to share they will also usually be your most popular thoughts or those that help to define you. There's no value in trying to please everyone, so if what you are making is attracting haters, take it as a good sign, not a bad one.

A great example of a personal brand based around a story is **Emily Rose**. Her brand and mission emerged after struggling to maintain meaningful relationships. It was causing her pain, and holding her back from living the life she wanted. Once discovering the root of her problem, she has the course to share her story and help others overcome this issue.

"In 2008 I read a book that basically slapped my spirit across its ephemeral face. I learned that my pattern of hopping from one relationship to the next in search of the high that comes from new attraction stunted my spiritual growth like any addiction does...

Realizing I had to change—if not to meet my soul mate, at least to embrace a life of spontaneity and have a passion-packed existence—a thirst for knowledge and spiritual growth emerged, and over the years I've managed to construct a life filled with luxury, travel, and blissful partnerships."

Be careful what you share and what gets shared about you.

Remember that once something is online, it is very difficult to control where it goes. Doing something "ugly" like talking bad about someone, posting photos of yourself or others doing illegal or immoral activities, or even writing a nasty email can come back to bite you. .

You also never know where these items will show up. A picture of you at a party may end up being the cover photo of a Business Insider article called "colleges where students work hard and party hard." (Yeah, it happened to me… at least I can say I was "Featured" on Business Insider.)

So generally, be kind to others (especially when online). Try to avoid publishing or sharing anything that you may regret 5-10 years down the road.

Associate with other strong brands

An easy way to gain recognition is to attach yourself to already strong brands. In later chapters I'll outline many strategies for reaching out to businesses, thought leaders and influencers in order to build your personal brand.

For now, it's important to understand that by aligning yourself with strong brands you'll borrow on their authority. Most of the traffic that will come to your site early on will come from other sites linking to yours. Make an effort to appear on other websites that discuss topics related to your brand. Contribute to your university's newsletter. Write a guest post for your current job's blog.

This could also mean speaking at events or hosting workshops. Start small and build up your communication and public speaking skills. You may not get big engagements at first, but if you start practicing early and often, more and more opportunities will start to flow. Your university is an excellent place to organize small events and get some experience speaking.

Key Takeaways

- Your personal brand is a valuable asset that can pay off in many unexpected ways.
- Your personal brand will be the platform to help you launch and share everything you create and will attract people who want to help you succeed.

- Start thinking of yourself as a brand; decide what qualities and ideas you want to be recognized for.
- Start by creating a simple website with your name as the domain.
- Tell your story by creating content on your website about the lessons you are learning or the thoughts you are having. Try to help other people with your ideas.
- Be careful what you share; once something is on the internet, it is hard to take down.

Chapter 8

KEY SKILLS FOR ENTREPRENEURS

I remember updating my resume when preparing to graduate with my Bachelor's. I was nearing the end of classes, and just a few finals were between me and "freedom."

Freedom…?

I had my doubts about that. It didn't seem like trading classes for a cubicle was a step toward freedom. But what other choice did I have?

So I went to the library and found a quiet corner to write out all the reasons why I would make a good employee.

I opened up a template resume and began to fill in the easy parts.

My name is Kyle… I'll put that at the top. Alight, that looks good, onward!

The silence of the library crept in around me. I felt like I could hear my own heart beating. The empty white space on the paper felt like a black hole.

I have a Bachelor's degree in International Studies… Is that a skill? It felt hollow all by itself.

I speak Spanish… That's useful, let's put that on there.

By now my heart beat started to sound more like rolling thunder.

I dug deeper.

I've got it! I'm proficient in Microsoft Word! That's important, right?

Alright… How about adding in a few words to describe myself…

How about "Driven by curiosity and excitement for discovery of new pathways."

What does that even mean?

Well I like to travel, I have lived in a few different countries. Is that something? Nah… employers would probably hate that.

Hmmmm… I think I'm in trouble here...

Nothing to show

Many students graduate with an education yet with no actual skills. Most of the concepts that you learn while acquiring a college degree are very theoretical. Students who spend all of their time in a classroom are often uncompetitive in the job market or in creating a business.

Building a business will help you develop skills that are universally desired and useful, whether you continue to be an entrepreneur for life, or join a larger organization. Building these skills will also create tangible results; you'll be able to cite specific ways you've used these skills and quantify the results you got. Through the process of learning these practical skills, it's unlikely you'll need to write a resumé at all; opportunities will seek you out instead of the other way round.

The primary skill

The most important skill is learning how to learn. The faster you can learn, the faster you can build other skills and reap the benefits. The world is changing quickly so being able to learn quickly will keep you ahead of the curve.

The best way to learn quickly is to develop a deep understanding of yourself.

Figure out what motivates you and use that to drive your learning. Find ways to reward yourself for your learning to cultivate a habit and a routine. Experiment to figure out the environment that you learn best in.

Don't trick yourself into thinking that once school is finished the learning is too. Continuing to learn and grow after you graduate is crucial for happiness and success. There is always something more to learn and improve on, even if you don't get course credit for it.

Learn by example

The skills below will vary in importance depending on your own inherent talents and the business model you choose to pursue. So you will need to them according to your needs.

One of the best ways to discover what skills will be most valuable is to get in contact with a role model. If you completed the exercise in "Chapter 5: Who do you want to be" you should have plenty of ideas for who to contact.

Many people are happy to share about and reflect on the skills had the biggest impact on their lives and businesses. You can learn a lot from the successes and failures of others who have businesses similar to the one you want to create. If you interview them as a student they won't feel like they are giving away their secrets to a competitor.

Remember to take these interviews with a grain of salt as well. Each individual's situation was likely different than yours; the exact strategy that worked for them may not work for you. And, even though someone is successful, it may be difficult for that person to completely explain why he/she was successful or that individual might attribute success to the wrong things. This is called **Survivorship Bias**. Their advice should serve as a rough guideline to help give you some direction.

Elective hours

Though many of the skills listed below come from experience and sweat, many universities will offer classes that can help you get an early start on them. Taking these classes is an excellent way to fill elective hours that are required for graduation, yet not strictly prescribed.

If the specific classes you are looking for aren't offered, there are often clubs on campus or meetups in your city that focus on these skills and have a community of people that are interested in developing them. Surrounding yourself with others who are interesting in growing the same skills as you are is a great way to learn faster and to have the accountability to stay on track.

10 basic skills for entrepreneurs

Focus: This skill is increasingly rare and valuable. Focus is important on multiple levels. The more you cultivate your ability to maintain focus on a single project for several hours at a time, the faster you will learn, build skills and develop ideas into something interesting.

It is important to understand that focus works in a very similar way to sleep. You fall asleep in stages, and to reach the deepest state of sleep usually takes somewhere between 25-45 minutes. If the cycle gets interrupted, you need to start over.

This is the same with focus. It may seem like a quick check of your facebook is harmless and only takes 30 seconds, but it actually costs you 25 minutes and 30 seconds. Whether it's with schoolwork, or building a business, an hour of completely focused work is worth far more than 4 hours of distracted and scattered work.

Comfort with uncertainty: Life as an entrepreneur has a great deal of uncertainty. Some months you may have victories and make a good income, others may be sparse. You may be the only person that really believes in what you are creating. You may have haters that try to bring you down; your friends and family may think you're crazy.

Nobody is truly an overnight success, although it is easier for us to imagine entrepreneurial stories in that light. There are often years of hard work and struggle that go unnoticed. Your success will depend on how well you tolerate this struggle and uncertainty. This is something every entrepreneur faces, and it is the price we pay for taking responsibility for the direction of our lives. Most people give up too early.

Listening and empathy: To be successful you must tune in to the needs of your customers. You must listen to them to understand what they want and need. You must have the empathy to understand their problems and to find a solution for them. Your empathy will not only guide you to create a better product or service, but it will help your sales and marketing by enabling you to craft a message that resonates with them.

You'll not only need to listen to your customers, but to your peers, team members, and mentors. As you grow a business you will constantly be facing new challenges and developing new skills. It's impossible for you to be a master of everything, so you must learn to have the humility to seek guidance from others.

Being able to "tune in" to the minds of your customers and identify unique needs that they face can empower you to break into even the most competitive of markets.

Writing: To many, this skill seems antiquated and irrelevant. However, writing remains one of the most powerful skills you can develop. Being able to clearly develop and express an idea is a tool for reaching thousands of people and demonstrating your knowledge. With the advent of blogging, it has never been easier to reach people with your writing. Blogging has removed many barriers that previously restricted people from reaching an audience. A simple, well-written blog filled with your ideas can be a platform for many opportunities.

Don't think that because your college papers are getting passing grades you have already mastered writing. Writing a paper that will be read once by a professor and writing an article that will be seen by thousands of people over time are two very different things. Not to mention that writing a paper on a pre-determined topic with strict guidelines is much simpler than coming up with your own topic and deciding the appropriate length, tone and context for your work. The world holds much harsher critics and much greater rewards than your university classes.

Public speaking: Being able to stand in front of a group of people with confidence and share an idea is one of the most powerful ways to connect with others. Even in the hyper-connected world of modern technology, face-to-face interactions are always more powerful avenues for spreading ideas.

A good place to hone your public speaking skills is **Toastmasters**, they have clubs and meetings in many cities around the world. There are also dozens of opportunities to speak on campus. There are often public speaking competitions held with cash prizes, or student-run clubs that may resonate with your ideas and allow you to speak. We'll talk more about this in later chapters.

Managing money / taxes: You'll need to be able to wisely manage the money you earn from your business. It can be tempting to spend early earnings on yourself, but you need to be sure you are re-investing to grow your business. Having the right mindset with money will be a big factor in how you manage your business.

You also need to make sure you are well organized and prepared for taxes. Keep track of your spending and earnings and have some money saved for when tax season comes around.

Sales: Even if you have something great to offer the world, you'll need to be able to convince people to buy it. The more expensive your product, the more important your sales skills.

The word "sales" often conjures up the image of a sleazy used car salesman using deceptive tactics to make a quick buck. But sales can be a very different process than that. Your ability to sell your product builds on your listening and empathy skills; you need to ask questions of the customer you are targeting, developing an understanding of what problem they want solved, and then to present your product or service as the solution.

Much of this ability can come from a quiet self-confidence and a firm belief in the the value of what you have to offer.

A good book to reference to start learning the basics of sales is **SPIN Selling**.

Relationship-Building: You could have the best business idea in the world, but without a strong network of people to help you it's not likely that your idea will go very far. Being able to build meaningful relationships will be critical to opening up new opportunities and advancing your business.

Most people try to open a relationship by asking for something. Most people that you admire and would want to connect with are bombarded with requests to "pick their brains". They have learned to "tune out" these requests entirely. By focusing on value you can add to other people's lives first, you can create a personal connection that will pay off in the future.

A fundamental read for networking is: "**How To Win Friends and Influence People**" by Dale Carnegie

Search Engine Optimization: 3.5 billion searches go through Google every day. Search engine optimization is the ability to get your site to show up first when people search for keywords relating to something you offer. Being able to capture this stream of searches and direct them to your website is one of the most powerful ways to build awareness of your business.

This skill seems highly technical, and the advanced techniques certainly are, but understanding the basics is easier than you think. One of the best resources for learning the basics of SEO is **Moz**.

Web design (HTML/CSS): Though it is easier than ever to build a website, knowing the basics of HTML and CSS can empower you to customize and maintain your site without having to hire an expensive developer every time you want to make a small change. Many drag-and-drop tools allow you to work on a site without the use of code, but to truly control the look and feel of your website, you'll want to have the basics down.

I predict that in 20 years being able to code will be as important as literacy.

Codeacademy is an excellent place for free lessons on the basics of code. Start with HTML and CSS, and if you find coding enjoyable try some of the more complex languages.

Negotiation: Most people are very uncomfortable with negotiation. It feels like conflict. But having a basic understanding of negotiation is critical to help you through some of the biggest decisions in your life like buying a house, resolving an argument with a significant other or working with a business partner.

The best place to start is a book called: **Crucial Conversations**

Understanding and interpreting data: In an online business, data is your compass. Without it, it is hard to navigate the waters of the internet. Your ability to collect data on how people are interacting with your website will give you key information for how you can improve your product and marketing.

Google Analytics is a free tool that is a standard on most websites. It gives you information about how many people visited your website, how they arrived, and what they looked at. Google offers a free course on the fundamentals of Google Analytics called **Analytics Academy.**

Why be a "jack of all trades"

You probably won't be able to master all of these skills. here will be a few that you gravitate to. Some will end up bringing you better results than others, and once you identify what those are you should focus your time and effort there.

I still recommend having at least a basic understanding of all of them. As you are starting out you'll be responsible for most of the tasks involved with these skills yourself. As your company grows you'll be able to hand off some of these skills to other people on your team, but if you don't have a basic understanding of them, you won't know what to look for in a team member or be able to tell the difference between a novice and an expert.

Key Takeaways

- Students who spend all of their time in a classroom often only learn theoretical skills, which aren't competitive in business or the job market.
- The most important skill is learning how to learn.
- Consider the skills people you admire have used to get the results you want.
- Leverage your elective hours to take courses that help build key entrepreneurial skills.
- You'll only be able to master a few of the skills listed in this chapter, but it is important to have a basic knowledge of all of them.

Chapter 9

EASY ONLINE BUSINESS MODELS

One of the biggest things that held me back from starting a business was my own mindset. I thought I needed to have an incredibly unique idea that had never been done before. But time kept passing and the idea never came. I decided to take action and try my hand at some business models that others had been successful with and that seemed promising.

I tried a few different businesses to see what would be a good fit for me. I tried creating an online store that sold custom leather jackets, but I realized I didn't like fashion nearly enough to continue with that model. I tried to create an online store that sold fire pits. I enjoyed creating and designing the site, but fire pits didn't capture my interest enough for me to stick with it for long.

When researching ways to market these businesses I learned about Conversion Rate Optimization (CRO). This process is a mix of art and science, running experiments with the design and messaging of a site to see how changes impact the behavior of people visiting the page. This fascinated me, and I thought I had a good taste for design and could find ways to improve sites for many different businesses.

I started by reading as many blog articles and case studies about CRO as I could find and after a few weeks I started calling this my specialty. It was not long before I found someone willing to let me do work on their site. I worked for free but they paid for the tools I wanted to use. Through this arrangement, I got some experience and my first case study. I came across new projects and started charging and then raising my prices.

I had finally found a business model that worked for me. But this is not something I would have discovered if I had continued waiting for the idea to pop into my head.

What kind of business should you start?

There are a few models that are easy to start without much cash or prior experience in business. You can run businesses from your laptop without a dedicated office space or lots of overhead costs. Depending on your skills, interests, and who you want to work with, some of these will be better fits than others. Some models focus on helping other businesses, and others focus on developing customers. Some of these models will help you develop a professional network while others will focus on building a brand and a following of fans and customers.

As you can see from my story, you may have to experiment with a few different models to before you find something that is a good fit for you. Don't be afraid to fail a few times; as long as you come away with a lesson, then failure is a key step in progressing to a business that you can be successful with. The important thing is to start, because that brilliant business idea will never appear if you don't take action to go out and find it.

Design

There is an increasing demand for design services online. There are endless ways to find a unique angle on design. You can choose to design websites, graphics for websites, animated videos, photography and much more. You can further differentiate yourself by targeting a specific industry and combining that with your skill. This is where you can mix your practical skills with your passion.

Maggie Appleton is a designer who found a niche for her creative work by providing unique illustrations for blog content and conferences. Visual content is a powerful element of marketing and social media. Unique visual content is highly valued on high traffic blogs. Take a look at one of the illustrations she created for the article "**How Do You Organize Your Time When**

You Don't Have a 9 to 5?"

Here's a few more examples of some interesting design businesses you could create:
- Web design for independent filmmakers
- Branding for yoga studios
- Animated explainer videos for apps

Create an online portfolio where you can display your work. Start small with projects for yourself and doing free work for local businesses. These can be leveraged for profitable work in the future.

The innovative product

Creating a new product is easier than you may think. Recent innovations like crowdfunding, 3D printing, and online retail has made it possible to quickly innovate on a product. Students have the advantage of fresh perspective and can find unique ways to improve that established businesses may have missed.

MadeReal.sg is a student-founded, student-run business that provides a subscription service for healthy snacks. The founders Roslyn and Robyn wanted to provide an easy way for healthy food producers to provide alternatives to the processed foods that are so pervasive in modern diets. Their subscription model makes it possible to compete with large brands without having to get on grocery store shelves.

If you have a good idea for an innovative product and a prototype to demonstrate it, you can create a crowdfunding campaign to spread the word about the product and get people to pay for it before it is made. Use that money to fund your development and manufacturing. The two big platforms for crowdfunding are **Kickstarter** and **Indiegogo**.

There are great examples of innovative product businesses started by students and financed by crowdfunding.

Soul Poles
Quantum Chess
Power Practical

Marketing services

If you have aspirations of creating or working in a fast-paced startup, a good place to start is by creating a marketing services business. Working with other businesses is also usually higher-valued work than working directly with customers. If you are talented, you can make a good profit from these skills as well. Here are a few ways you could specialize to help businesses:

- **Social Media Marketing** - As a young college student you are probably on the cutting edge of social media trends. Businesses are always looking for help building social media presence on new platforms and getting a competitive advantage there. The followers you help attract to a businesses' social media page can turn into customers later.
- **Search Engine Optimization (SEO)** - When you search for something in a search engine like Google, there is a system that determines which sites appear at the top of the page. The closer it is to the top of the list on the front page, the more traffic will come to a website. SEO is the process of making a site appear higher on those lists.
- **Content Marketing** - One of the most powerful ways for a brand to build a relationship with its customers is to create content that is interesting and helpful. Many businesses are desperate to create content that will attract customers to their websites. Content can be blog posts, social media, videos, infographics and much more.
- **Conversion Rate Optimization** - If 100 people visit a website in a day

and 10 of them end up purchasing a product, you'll have a conversion rate of 10%. Conversion Optimization is the practice of understanding design and persuasion and finding ways to improve how people experience a website to increase that percentage.

- **Email Marketing** - Many businesses value having a sequence of emails that they can automatically send to potential customers. These emails might educate people about a product or service or work to persuade people to purchase that product.
- **Paid Traffic** - Being able to drive traffic to a website on demand is something almost every business with a web presence wants. With tools like Facebook Ads and Google AdWords you can drive traffic to specific pages to capture leads and customers for businesses.

It is easy to learn the basics of a marketing skill and to be useful to small businesses and startups. You may ask yourself "If it is easy for me to learn, why would a business not already have it?" Business owners are constantly confronted with problems and challenges, they don't have the time or the resources to learn and do everything for themselves. That's why, even as a beginner, you can make a big impact with businesses.

Some resources to help you start to learn these skills are **Digital Marketer** (they offer courses with certifications) and **Udemy**.

Personal development / Coaching / Tutoring

If you are a great teacher or coach in a certain area there is a lot of opportunity to build a brand around that skill and create a business. The best place to start is by examining your own story. What challenges have you overcome in your life? Where can you help people?

You do not need to teach something technical or complicated, it just needs to be interesting and have a unique twist to it. You could teach anything from cooking, to fitness or gaming, travel, dating, language learning, happiness, study habits and plenty more. If it is a skill people can get better at, then there is a market for a teacher.

You can attract students by creating interesting and helpful content like video tutorials for workouts or a detailed blog post about how you overcame a challenge and with action steps for others to follow.

The key with this model is to find an interesting way to differentiate yourself from the other established brands. A good example of this is Zachary Stockill's **Overcoming Retroactive Jealousy blog.** There are thousands of blogs on building better relationships, and Zachary honed in on a very specific problem that had previously not been well-defined or explored.

One common way people make money through this model of business is through creating and teaching courses. A good place to start with online courses is **Udemy**. They make it easy to host a course and have a huge community of students active on the site. Udemy will also help promote your course and indirectly drive traffic to your website.

A book is an excellent product for a coach to sell in order to build their brand. Instructive books don't need to be very long and you don't need to be an amazing writer to have a successful book. In fact, people like short books that get right to the point and are easy to apply to their lives. For guides on writing and publishing your own book, I recommend checking out **Self-Publishing School.**

Often before you can start selling products you need to build up your brand and get a following. This process can take a long time. It's not unreasonable to expect that it may take a year or more of creating content for free; it takes this time and effort to start accumulating followers and building enough trust with them before you start to see income. This may seem like a tremendous amount of time invested, but once your brand has traction you'll have a source of income based on your passion. This is why it is so important to start early.

Be careful with business partners

It's a tempting idea to start a business with a friend. You have someone to bounce ideas off, and someone to share the workload with. Perhaps you and your friend have different skillsets that complement each other. But remember that a business partnership is a complex and important relationship.

If you are going into business with a partner, make sure you have your partnership detailed in writing. Even if things are starting small, it's very easy for a relationship to be ruined by a disagreement around a business when you don't have a contract established.

Fill out the right paperwork

Once you get to the point where you are charging for your services it is good to make sure you have your business registered. Forming a small business and getting the proper licenses to sell products (if necessary) should only take a day or two and usually cost less than $100.

Key Takeaways

- These four models are far from the only options out there, but these should serve as a good springboard for experimentation.
- Your idea may not be fully formed when you set out, but testing out these models and learning as you go will teach you about yourself and give you more direction over time.

- If there's a model that interests you but you don't have the skills yet, don't be afraid to invest in learning the basics. Paying for a course or a tool is like placing a bet on yourself, and there's few better bets you can make.
- Don't be afraid to abandon a model that is not working for you.s long as you continue to try new things and seek out a business that you can stick with in the long run.

PART 3

How to make your university work for you

Chapter 10

SIMPLE WAYS TO BE MEMORABLE AND BUILD RELATIONSHIPS

I was about halfway through a semester long exchange in Cordoba, Argentina. It was one of the best semesters in my college career. I loved the people, the place, and what I was learning both in and out of the classroom.

I owed a great deal of this experience to Jesse, the advisor in my study abroad office. He worked hard to help me find a location to study that suited me, and connected me with a few other students that had just returned from there. I decided to send a brief "thank you" email to Jesse letting him know I was having a great time and thanking him for his help in setting this up for me. I added links to a few videos I had made to share my experience with friends and family.

He responded that in 10 years working as an advisor he had never received a thank you email out of the blue like that. He shared the videos with many of his contacts across the university.

That simple "thank you" went a long way in building a relationship that would be a tremendous benefit to me in the future. A few years later, I was applying for my first job after completing my undergraduate degree; I was applying to be a study abroad advisor myself. Although by that time Jesse moved on from the office, he was willing to help me with my application, give me a recommendation and give me an insider's perspective of how to succeed.

Without that simple "thank you" email, I'm not sure I would have landed that job a few years later.

How to be memorable and build relationships

You can never anticipate how or when you will benefit from the relationships you develop--they unfold in ways that you can't predict. But at certain key times, a relationship you have can completely change the course of your life.

Since you can't predict how the relationships in your life will benefit you, it's best to plant as many seeds as possible and simply trust that you will be rewarded down the line for your actions.

Listed below are simple ways to build relationships. You can use these techniques for people on campus or in your community. Many of these techniques can be used online as well if you are interested in reaching out to someone who is far away.

Be Helpful

Think of small ways you may be able to help people out. Help a professor clean up the lab after class. Send an interested student their way. Each small act of generosity will come back tenfold in ways you could not imagine.

Don't worry about getting compensated for the value you add. You should trust that the rewards for building relationships will come in the future and may not come in the form of something you're expecting or are even aware of right now. The relationship itself and the trust you build will open doors to more interesting and serendipitous opportunities in the future.

In her TED talk "**Be an opportunity maker**", Kare Anderson encourages the audience to become opportunity makers.

"When you connect with people around a shared interest and action, you're accustomed to serendipitous things happening into the future".

The options for adding value will vary depending on the person you want to connect with. At first, you may not feel like you have much to offer the people around you with whom you would like to connect. But as a young student you have at least one thing to offer that is incredibly valuable: your time, energy and willingness to learn.

Most of the people you'll want to build relationships with (professors, entre-preneurs, thought leaders, scientists, etc.) will probably be short on time and energy, and most people who reach out to them probably want to take more of their time without offering anything in return. If you can find a way to to help them, then you will stand out from 99% of the people they interact with.

Make a habit to spend 30 minutes each day brainstorming how you could help someone and add value to their lives.

Catch up periodically

Building relationships on campus and off takes time. Make sure to keep up with professors and academic advisors by visiting them every few months and catching up. Visit them during their office hours and let them know what you are up to. Try to come equipped with some news or ideas that might be interesting to them. Have you read a good book or article that relates back to some coursework you did with them? How have you been applying what you learned in their class to your life?

Take the opportunity to get to know them as well. Ask them about their lives outside of work. What are their hobbies, passions or aspirations? And remember, always be searching for ways that you can help them or add value. Your help can even be something trivial and unrelated to your work; if your professor isn't sure what to cook for dinner tonight, send her a recipe for one of your favorite dishes.

If you can't meet in person it's still worthwhile to send periodic email updates.

I have a template tool to help you keep track of and manage your relation-ships, you can download it at Kylegray.io/resources.

Send a thank you card

When you were a kid your mom probably forced you to write thank you cards to your friends and family for every birthday present you received. It happened to me. At the time it felt like pulling teeth. But like most things, you come to see the wisdom in your parents' decisions later in life.

Taking a moment to share gratitude is absolutely powerful. Send your thanks to anyone who helps you with a quick card. This is something that is done so infrequently it is a tragedy. Any time someone helps you is an opportunity to say "thank you." By showing gratitude you invite more of the same into your life and you make an impact on the person who helped you.

You can have an even bigger impact with a handwritten note. It does not have to be very long to make a big impression. The process of writing out and sending notes shows that you took some time out of your day to appreciate what someone has done for you. Make sure to always leave the door open for you to return the favor if they need help.

Your note could be as short as two sentences:

"Dear [person],
Thank you for [the thing they did for you], because of your help [describe how your life is better because of what they did].

Please let me know if there's anything I can do for you in return.

Cheers,

[your name]"

Ask their advice

Asking for advice is a great way to build a relationship. You get to stroke their ego a little bit and give them the satisfaction of helping someone.

If you want to reach out to a professor, advisor or someone on campus, you can usually ask their advice straight away. If there is someone you want to reach out to off campus, like a business owner or thought leader, it may be better to start a conversation by adding value first before you ask their advice.

Don't be overbearing or vague when you ask for advice. The average entrepreneur is constantly bombarded with emails of people requesting to "pick their brains" about half-baked business ideas. A good way to frame asking for advice is to build the questions you want to ask into a project you are working on for school. Then reach out to the person and ask if you can ask them some questions related to a paper you are working on.

Connect people

As you grow your network you will undoubtedly meet people with varied skills and interests. One of the most valuable things you can do is to connect others in a helpful way.

Connecting people who share similar ideas and passions positions you as a leader and helps spread ideas. The two people you connect with benefit from each other and will also credit you for the help they have received even if you only made a simple introduction. Best of all, you are adding value and making a big impact on two people simultaneously. So not only is this one of the most powerful ways to help people and be a leader, but you are doubling that effect.

So as you meet new people with whom you want to build relationships, always be asking yourself "Who do I know that this person would love to meet?"

Engage online

Perhaps you want to reach out to someone off-campus, outside of your city or state. There are many ways to plant the seeds for good relationships online.

Social media - Look up their social media channels. What topics are they passionate about? Try to find content that they might be interested in and share it with them. Add your take on the article or ask a question to start a conversation.

Blogs - Do they have a blog? Leave some in-depth comments on a few of their posts. If they have a "how-to" article or a guide, test out their process and then respond with your experience. You could even take it a step further and create a play-by-play of you carrying out their guide on your own blog.

You could also find a way to tie this back into your schoolwork. We'll discuss this is more detail in later chapters, but I recommend taking classes that would allow you some freedom in choosing a topic for a paper or a project. With this freedom you can set up your schoolwork as a tool to build relationships.

If they have a product or a service that you use, you could create a post or a video reviewing it. Describe what worked best for you, or maybe give some suggestions on how it could be improved. Create something that they would be excited to share on their social media accounts or website.
Share your experience / become an advocate

A common mistake people make while trying to grow a business or a brand online is reaching out to influencers and asking for something right away.

They don't open by adding value. One of the easiest ways to connect with someone is to become an advocate for them.

This can work with people you want to reach out to online, but also remember that many organizations on campus are starved for good social media content, reviews, or anything they can share that is related to them.

- **Create videos** - Creating short videos about an experience can make you unforgettable and get you noticed.
- **Write a review** - A good review or summary of an experience or project is something that can be used for future students regarding a program on campus
- **Volunteer** - Many organizations on campus have events that need volunteers. See if you can lend a hand or help them promote the event.

The exponential power of your network

The network you build will be the main avenue for feeding you opportunities, growing your business and brand. Your network will increase in power as you deepen your existing relationships, but also as you get to know new people. Things may start small, but if you persist in helping people and building relationships, you should start to experience a snowball effect. Be patient in the early stages, and you will be greatly rewarded.

These strategies for building relationships are fundamental in being successful in almost all of the strategies following this chapter.

Key takeaways

- Relationships can unfold in ways that you can't predict, so be generous and trust that you'll be rewarded in the future.

- The key to building good relationships is focusing on how you can add value and create opportunities for the other person, not for yourself.
- A handwritten thank you card is a powerful way to show gratitude and invite future positive interactions.
- As your network grows, try to connect people that can help each other.

Chapter 11

YOUR KEY TO CAMPUS: ACADEMIC ADVISORS

During my first year as a student, the university seemed like a well-organized machine working toward one goal: educating students. The large buildings, lively campus and students rushing in every direction made it look like everyone had a place on campus and knew it well. Things seemed to have a harmony and a consistency. It was both comforting and intimidating.

This illusion persisted in many ways until I graduated with my bachelors.

Because of many of the connections I had made on campus I managed to get a job as an advisor in the study abroad office. I was in charge of all study abroad programs going to Latin America, Africa, the Middle East and Spain. I worked with professors from many different colleges within the university. I also was responsible for the marketing for our office and worked on building partnerships with many other offices on campus like the student government, veterans' affairs, and the disability center. Only then did I realize the truth about the campus.

Behind the scenes, the university was not the well-oiled machine I thought it to be as a student. It was more like a group of medieval kingdoms like a chapter from Game of Thrones. There was the kingdom of business and the kingdom of engineering competing for students, new buildings and prestige. Some were more powerful than others. Professors were knights vying for academic recognition and the all-important blessings of 'tenure.'

I too had to work to gain favor and attention for the study abroad office. I had to learn to navigate the different rivalries and agendas to advance my own causes. I learned who to go to if I wanted help organizing events, and how certain professors liked to be addressed.

As a student, this may seem disconcerting to you. The institution that you have invested so much of your time and money into is very different than you expected, and you best interests aren't always the top priority.

But this is good news. If you can learn to see the university landscape like this and understand the motivations of different people and organizations on campus, you can use this knowledge to your advantage. You'll learn certain people can help you while others will just waste your time. A "no" from one person on an idea could be a resounding "yes" from another.

But how can you develop your understanding of campus? The first step is to build a relationship with an academic advisor.

The benefits of a good academic advisor

I recommend building a relationship with an academic advisor as early as possible in your academic career.

You may have been assigned an advisor right as you entered the university. But remember that you can choose your advisor and work with several at the same time. Experiment with advisors in your department until you find someone you really resonate with. If you have multiple majors or minors then you'll have more to work with.

Having a good academic advisor is extremely valuable. They can help you with obvious things such as planning out which courses you will take to fulfill graduation requirements. But we both know you're looking beyond that. Let your advisor know about your goals for starting a business before you graduate, and that you are looking for ways that the university can help you. You'll want to know about more than what classes are available; your advisor can help you understand what programs are out there to support you.

Here's a few ways they may be able to help:

They know the campus - An advisor has a completely different perspective of the campus than a student. They understand the inner workings of the campus. Though they expect to help students choose classes, they can help you navigate the university and achieve your goals as well.

They know alumni and peers with similar interests - It's unlikely that you are the only student who wants to start a business or has the passions you have. An academic advisor meets and works with hundreds of students over the course of a year and may be able to connect you with students and alumni who have accomplished goals similar to yours.

They know faculty - They know which professors teach what classes, the personalities of the professors, and what their goals and motivations are. They'll know which ones might be open to working with a motivated student (like you) who wants to do something unique while at university.

They know where the power centers on campus are - Power centers are places that are growing more quickly than the rest of the university and have a large amount of funding. They tend to have many programs, opportunities and scholarships for students who work with them. Even if these power centers don't immediately seem to be connected to your interests, they may have resources or programs that could help you.

They know where to find funding opportunities - Scholarships are only the beginning of opportunities to obtain funding. There are many other ways to finance your business (which we will discuss in later chapters). Your advisor can help connect you with the right people to get this funding.

Don't expect to have a perfect picture of the campus and it's opportunities after just one meeting with an advisor. And don't expect them to give you all the details they know right away. Like everything in this book, these things take time.

Build relationships with a few advisors around campus and meet with them once or twice a semester. Keep them updated on your goals and progress and thank them if you use their advice and it comes in handy. As you continue to meet with them and show that you aren't a student who just wants to coast through your education, they will start to share more opportunities with you and think of you first when new ones appear.

Key Takeaways

- Remember that you can choose your advisor, you don't have to stick with the one you are assigned to.
- You should build relationships with different advisors across your university, they will know of different resources to help you with your goals.
- Advisors can help you with more than just picking out classes; they understand the campus and can help you find opportunities, resources, like-minded students and professors you would get along with.

Chapter 12

INCREASE YOUR OPTIONS WITH A FLEXIBLE OR CUSTOM MAJOR

As a graduate student I chose an interdisciplinary degree that would give me access to various colleges and their resources. It was called a Master's in International Affairs and Global Enterprise, or **MIAGE**. I was able to pick and choose from courses in the Law, MBA, and Social Science programs at my university. This gave me the chance to get access to opportunities and resources that each of these different colleges offered without having to commit to many of the obligations of the individual programs.

I was able to piece together classes that I thought were interesting and would benefit me in the future. I combined negotiation and mediation training from the law school with social entrepreneurship from the business school. This also helped to broaden my network since I regularly interacted with students and professors from all of these different programs.

I also found that the administration was receptive to the idea of "customized coursework." I wanted to free up some time to work on my business while still progressing toward graduation so I began to look for ways I could combine classes with building by business.

With some hard work and carefully building relationships with the administration and faculty in my program, I was able to get professors to agree to allow me to do "directed readings" about starting an international business. I provided weekly reports of what I learned and how it applied to the program and summarized my learnings in a long-form paper at the end of the semester.

I learned about outsourcing, remote work, and marketing and sales through building out my own business and doing free work for companies. I was happy to trade free work for experience working with startups, recommendations, and for content for my weekly reports.

By the end of the semester with my "directed readings," I had a case study about how I helped a business improve their marketing. I had hands-on experience working with businesses and a network of entrepreneurs that began referring me to paying customers.

Why add a flexible major or minor?

Your time at university is a time to explore different skills and opportunities. If you are in a major that has a very strict curriculum you may be restricting what's available to you and your access to resources.

I recommend selecting an interdisciplinary program as your main field of study. These programs are becoming more and more common across the US and Europe. If you are interested in developing well-defined and technical skills such as engineering, computer science, or physics then consider an interdisciplinary minor to accompany your major.

An interdisciplinary major gives you more control over your education and allows you more flexibility in choosing courses that are relevant to you and your goals. You'll also be more able to avoid irrelevant courses that are requirements for more focused degrees.

Adding a flexible major or minor allows you to explore different areas of your university. This may make you eligible for different scholarships, internships or other resources that are not available for your primary major.

Choose a major or minor related to the power centers on your campus to get access to their resources and networks.

A flexible field of study means you may be able to meet faculty, students, and administration from various schools and departments. A flexible field of study is more likely to have a professor whot you can partner with to create custom classes to help you grow your business.

It's important to consider that adding another major or minor could increase the overall amount of work you need to do to graduate, and the amount of tuition you would have to pay. Especially if there's not much overlap between the coursework you would have to do for each of them. So make this decision carefully.

Do plenty of research before adding a major and get to know the faculty and staff that work with the program. Be forthcoming about your aspirations to start a business and talk with an advisor for the program to see if there would be opportunities to help you in your goals. Ask about scholarships, student jobs and programs that may help you get resources or experience relevant to your business.

Custom majors

Maybe you have searched already and can't find any degrees that suit your interests and focus on developing the skills you want.

In many large public universities, it is possible to create a custom major or minor. These custom programs allow students to pull coursework from different departments and arrange them into a degree relevant to their specific interests. If you understand the skills that are critical to your success in your business, you could consider actually building a major around those skills.

Check with your academic advisor to see of this is possible.

To give you a better idea of what's possible here's a list of previously approved programs of study form several universities across the US.

http://ugs.utah.edu/bus/examples.php
https://dornsife.usc.edu/student-designed-curricula
http://www.bradley.edu/academic/colleges/las/departments/imp/
http://www.scps.virginia.edu/degrees/degree-detail/
bachelor-of-interdisciplinary-studies

Learning to learn

Being exposed to a diverse set of courses and ideas will help you develop the most important skill to building your business, and succeeding in life in general: learning how to learn quickly. Challenging yourself with a wide array of topics will help you absorb new information and connect ideas in new ways.

Growing a business is a constant process of taking in new information and connecting the ideas and information in unique ways.
Taking your education into your own hands

With a flexible or customized major you'll have more power to direct your education. You'll be able to focus on the skills that are important and practical to develop for starting and growing your business.

You may be concerned that an interdisciplinary or custom major may not look as good on a resume or may seem less prestigious than more classical degrees. But consider that as an increasing percentage of the population is getting a degree, it is becoming more of a "minimum requirement" than a "golden ticket." Many organizations these days value experience, grit and creativity more than any individual degree.

Key Takeaways

- A flexible major can help you access the classes, skills and resources you need to grow your business.
- Picking a major or minor that is closely related to where the power centers on your campus are gives you access to unique programs and opportunities.
- If you can't find a major that works for you, you may be able to create a fully-customized major.

Chapter 13

CUSTOM COURSEWORK - HOW TO GET CREDIT
FOR WORKING ON YOUR BUSINESS

When I shared my aspirations to start a business, friends and colleagues at my university thought I was crazy. Most people wrote my goals off as a passing phase or quarter-life crisis. I wondered if they were right; I had not met anyone who had achieved what I wanted to and I often doubted if it was possible.

That all changed after a conversation with a professor. I was once again explaining my plan to build a skill and offer marketing services to businesses. I did not want to be rich, I just wanted to be free to run my business from anywhere. He responded with a calm and confident "That's a totally modest and achievable goal." I was floored by the statement. I was so used to being dismissed that this took me by surprise.

I explained in further detail how I had built a few websites that were collecting a small amount of money from people clicking on ads, and talked about a few other ideas I wanted to pursue. Over time I built a relationship with this professor, and asked if he would be willing to do "directed readings" with me. The directed readings would help me turn my business pursuits into course credit.

He agreed to meet with me weekly at a coffee shop if I agreed to make a strong effort to advance my businesses, connect with customers and record what I was doing each week. After working with my advisor I found a way to get credit for these meetings as well, which freed up time that I would usually be spending in a classroom to work on my business.

Though I did not have any assigned readings or homework, I had to find my own questions and my own answers. If I continued to make progress on my business and share what I was learning with him, he would continue to support me. Though he did not share any shortcuts to making my business work (because there aren't any) his support and guidance pointed me in the right direction.

How to create your own coursework with the help of a professor

If you are a self-directed student that is determined to grow a business, you may be able earn course credit for the work you are doing. This will help you graduate faster and possibly enable you to get access to other university resources. You'll also be able to receive individualized mentorship and guidance from a professor.

An obvious place to find a professor who will support your work is the business school at your university. Having a major or a minor in business should give you access to helpful classes and help you to find a professor who would be interested in working with you.

You'll need to be clever, finding a way to relate the work you are doing for your business to your coursework. Having a flexible or customized major or minor should also help you find professors who would be open to working with you on your business.

Find the right professor

Start by identifying a professor with a teaching style that you enjoy and who discusses topics closely related to your business. The best ones in this case are often "black sheep" professors: they're often younger, more rebellious and more energetic than other professors. These professors love to work with motivated students who want to do more than just daydream through class.

Talk to your professor a bit after class every once in a while or go to their office hours. Learn about them and help them get to know you and your goals. It helps to be performing well in class, but it is more important to show you care about your education and are willing to work hard--this will help build trust. We discussed in previous chapters' techniques and strategies to build relationships. Use those strategies to start conversations and get to know the professor you want to work with.

Keep in mind that many professors are overworked and strained for time. Building a relationship with them may take several months or even semesters. You should not be discouraged if they aren't open to working one-on-one with a student. Most universities aren't structured to incentivize this, so a professor will need to really like and trust you before. This will be a personal investment of time and energy on their part.

After you have taken time to build relationships with one or a few professors, ask if they would be willing to advise you on some "independent study" or "directed readings". These are common terms for custom coursework at most universities.

Tell them about the business you are working on and about your plan for starting or growing it. Here's an outline of what that plan should look like:

- Describe your business idea to them.
- Mention one to three problems related to the business that you would like to understand.
- List a few skills you will be studying and developing. Try to relate these skills to courses the professor teaches.
- Submit 1 paper a week on a topic related to the job or industry.
- Meet once a week with the professor to talk about the issues you uncover and what you are learning.
- At the end of the semester you will do a comprehensive presentation on what you have learned. Offer to arrange an event and invite students and professors to attend the presentation.

You will need to customize this plan according to the situation and who you would like to work with. The more detailed you can be in your plan, the better. Your plan could involve visiting and researching local businesses you would like to work with or that serve similar customers. Or if you have identified a problem you want to solve, you can propose it as a project.

Get help from your academic advisor

Your academic advisor should have a grasp of what it takes to set up an "independent study" course. As you are starting to create your plan for your own independent study, let your advisor know about what you are trying to do. They should be able to help you through the process and might even be able to direct you to professors who would be receptive to your idea.

You will likely only earn elective credit for this course and will still have to fulfill many core courses for graduation, but there's a slight chance you may be able to fill specific degree requirements from this work.

Make some progress on your own first

Don't wait for permission from a professor or an advisor to get started on your business. You need to be determined to make your business happen whether or not you are getting course credit for it in the process.

You'll have better luck with professors and advisors if you already have a start on your business before seeking credit for it. This will demonstrate that you are taking the process seriously and give some proof to that you are determined to make progress each week. You want to demonstrate that you are not simply using this as an opportunity to get course credit for nothing.

Key Takeaways

- It's possible to design your own course. Self-designed courses are usually referred to as directed readings. Create a course to help develop a skill related to your business.
- Build a relationship with a professor who would be likely to support your directed readings.
- Create a detailed plan and syllabus, outlining what you will learn and what you plan to do for this custom coursework. Make it as easy as possible for the professor to say "yes."
- Work with your advisor to create a plan and find a good professor.
- Don't be discouraged if your plan is rejected at first. Keep trying with different ideas and different professors.
- Get started on your project even if you don't get approved for custom coursework. Having a project that already has traction will make it easier to get your plan approved.

Chapter 14

FUND YOUR SKILL-DEVELOPMENT WITH UNDERGRADUATE RESEARCH

I was appalled… I was disgusted… I was … Ok, I'll admit it I was a bit jealous.

I was quite young for an advisor, and being fresh out of school myself I still very much identified with the students I worked with. This was a good thing when I was speaking with students, they trusted me and were more honest. I could give them straight answers in a way they understood. However, my age was sometimes a drawback with older faculty and staff.

I had to sit through many meetings where older people would gather together and pontificate about "Millennials:" how this generation thought, what they needed, how global warming was their fault because they text too much, and so on. I didn't enjoy these meetings very much. I felt like I was in a room full of people gossiping about me.

At least once a year most of the advisors were gathered together to update everyone on what was happening at the university. The new trend we were discussing this time was undergraduate research. Faculty involved with the undergraduate research program were boasting of the benefits of under-graduate research:

- Students actively learning by asking their own questions and finding the answers.
- Students learning how to conduct disciplined research and project management.
- Students collaborating with other students and their community, trying to solve problems and answer questions in their own "backyard."

Opportunities were open to students of all disciplines and interests, and large amounts of funding for scholarships and resources were being funneled to these programs.

My jaw dropped hearing these stories. A mix of emotions washed over me. I was at first astounded that this was a novel idea. Undergraduate students can think for themselves and direct their own research? This seemed so obvious to me. They are of age to fight wars, manage their own taxes, pay tuition, vote and start their own business. Of course they can conduct research that is valuable to the academic community, and more importantly to their local communities. Furthermore, there were many undergraduate students who weren't "millennials?" Many non-traditional students have years of valuable experience that could be plugged into programs like this. They're the future right? Of course they should be out there doing research on how to make it better.

As I cooled off I realized a lot of this righteous fury I was experiencing was fueled by envy. I was upset I had not heard about this opportunity before, that I did not get a shot at undergraduate research.

This was one of the many treasures I discovered as an advisor that I wish I would have known about as a student.

What is undergraduate research?

Undergraduate research is becoming increasingly popular at public universities. Many large universities are dedicating more resources and marketing efforts to promote these programs and encourage students to participate.

There is an opportunity here for students to get funding to do focused work understanding a problem and developing solutions for it. Most students are researching topics that have interested them for years. Others have found ways to take two subjects they have been studying and look for connections.

Consider how you could connect the work you want to do in your business to undergraduate research.

Why do undergraduate research?

Focused work on a problem that interests you: You choose what you will work on. This self-directed research will give you the chance to learn more about a problem or an idea that interests you. This understanding will help you understand how you can add value in an area and find opportunities to develop a business.

You can get access to funding to help facilitate your research: This money can cover expenses for equipment, travel and can help with some personal expenses. This will free up time for you to focus on your research instead of working a part time job to cover your bills.

Increased authority on a topic that interests you: Even if your work does not directly lead to the formation of a business, the time you spend deeply researching a problem will give you insights and many opportunities to share your ideas via publications, speaking opportunities and on your university's website.

Real-world experience managing a project and getting results: Conducting research means managing a budget, making decisions on how to invest your time and resources, and searching for unique and valuable ways to combine ideas and information. This in many ways is the same process as growing a business.

Mentorship from a professor: Most undergraduate research programs require working closely with a professor to help guide you through the process. A professor can help you strategize, overcome roadblocks and refine your ideas into something interesting.

How to start undergraduate research

Research whether or not your university has an undergraduate research program:

It may be easiest just to type the name of your university + undergraduate research in a search engine. But you can also ask your academic advisor and see if they are aware of any opportunities on your campus.

If you do have an an undergraduate research program at your university, make an appointment with an advisor or attend an information session to learn what opportunities are available and discover the details of the application process.

Get a basic idea for your research:

An easy way to start is by looking up past research projects to get an idea of what your university has approved and to get some inspiration for what's possible.

Universities may favor certain topics or fields of study over others. They also typically have different positions open each year for research related to specific topics. You'll want to find an opening that relates to your business idea. Some are very specific (3D printing fossil ammonite shells for hydrodynamic experiments) while others are broad and flexible (Business Research Projects).

It's a good idea to look at what has been approved at other universities (especially rival universities) to get a broader range of ideas and to have a precedent for your research if similar projects have been done with other universities.

Here's a list of some places where you can find some student stories:

- UCLA
- University of Washington
- Ohio State University
- University of Utah

Find a faculty mentor:

Find a professor who has a background related to the topic you want to research, and begin to develop a relationship with them. If they know you, they will be more likely to be willing to work with you on undergraduate research.

If you don't know where to start, ask faculty and advisors that you know well if they could connect you with a professor who might be interested in working with you.

Volunteer / Understand the problem:

To be approved for most undergraduate research programs you need to demonstrate an understanding in your chosen topic. Depending on the topic you want to research, there are many ways to demonstrate your understanding. One of the simplest ways is to write a short four-page paper on the topic to explain why it resonates with you.

Before you apply it is important that you have already started this research project. You want to demonstrate this is something you are passionate about and that you aren't just looking to get a handout.

Keep in mind this process may take a long time. Deadlines to apply are usually two months before the semester begins, and you need to be start planning your research and preparing several months in advance before you are approved.

Don't give up if you are turned down the first time:

Undergraduate research is a very new concept. Many universities have only been doing it for a few years and they don't always have everything figured out. If you pitch your idea but it is turned down, try and get some feedback and try again next time applications open. Do your best to strengthen your case between applications.

Key Takeaways

- Check with your advisor to see if undergraduate research is available at your university.
- See what research opportunities are available, or if it possible to propose your own.
- Find a professor to mentor you in your research.
- Make sure you have a good understanding of the problem before you pitch your research plan.
- Know the timelines for applications and try to plan as far in advance as possible.

Chapter 15

CREATE A TRIBE WITH A CLUB OR MEETUP

Wow. I found it…

A place where I don't feel crazy, or at least the people around me were as crazy as I was.

As my ideas for starting my own business began to solidify I learned about a program at my university called "The Foundry". The Foundry on paper was a business incubator, but there was no funding from venture capitalists being passed around, no guru secrets to successful startups. It was a place for people who wanted to become entrepreneurs to support each other on their journeys.

With only a small budget for snacks and a place to hold meetings, a tight community was formed. Some of the students in the Foundry were building six figure businesses, launching successful crowdfunding campaigns, and following their dreams. I was thrilled to have weekly meetings with people of all different ages, skills, and aspirations where we could discuss the challenges of growing a business.

Finally, I had a place where I could talk about the challenges I was facing. I felt so lonely trying to figure out everything on my own. Here I could help others and get help in return. Here I could share my victories and failures and be vulnerable about what I was going through.

I found my tribe.

The tribes we lead

In his TED talk called "**The Tribes We Lead**" Seth Godin talks about people's hunger to connect with ideas and leaders with a cause.

"You don't need permission from people to lead them. But in case you do, here it is: they're waiting, we're waiting for you to show us where to go next. So here is what leaders have in common. The first thing is, they challenge the status quo. They challenge what's currently there. The second thing is, they build a culture. A secret language, a seven-second handshake, a way of knowing that you're in or out. They have curiosity. Curiosity about people in the tribe, curiosity about outsiders. They're asking questions. They connect people to one another.

Do you know what people want more than anything? They want to be missed. They want to be missed the day they don't show up. They want to be missed when they're gone. And tribe leaders can do that. It's fascinating, because all tribe leaders have charisma, but you don't need charisma to become a leader. Being a leader gives you charisma. If you look and study the leaders who have succeeded, that's where charisma comes from -- from the leading. Finally, they commit. They commit to the cause. They commit to the tribe. They commit to the people who are there".

The same idea or passion that you have for fueling your business and/or personal brand can be the spark that creates a tribe. A tribe can start small, but it can have a powerful snowball effect and incite change. The small group of people that join your tribe early can become ambassadors for your idea and help you reach more and more people.

Why start a club on campus?

Building interest around an idea is one of the most powerful and needed forms of leadership in the world today. Starting a club can be your first step in building this skill.

There are few places more fertile for leaders to build tribes than a university. Campuses are filled with young people desperate to find meaning and purpose in their lives. Your idea does not have to be a world-changing idea, it just needs to build a culture around a shared interest or passion.

Even the focus of your club is not connected to your business, the leadership skills you develop will prove invaluable in growing your business in the future.

No matter how obscure your idea may be, there's almost certainly others on your campus who are interested as well. Even in the unlikely case that you are the first person on campus to have this interest, your passion is contagious. If you're willing to share your ideas, spread the word, and open yourself up to others about what you care about, you will inspire people to join you.

Universities encourage and support clubs. It's a constant challenge for many universities to keep students engaged with activities on campus. So when a student approaches them with a unique idea, work hard to support them. Depending on the number of members and how energized students are a university can provide thousands of dollars in funding for events, food, speakers, workshops, supplies and almost anything else that you can argue is aligned with the goals of the university.

Connect your club with your personal brand

Share the stories and discussions you have with your club on your website to build up your personal brand. The members of your club will become early advocates for what you are doing and will share your content online. This can help your idea expand from your campus to the world at large.

Communities and business

Many businesses thrive based on the communities they create and the people they lead. A sense of community attracts new customers to a business, and it also gives the business a direct way to interact with and learn from their customers, which helps build a better product or service. The community also builds an emotional connection with the business and increases loyalty to the business. So even if a competitor comes by with a cheaper product or a slight improvement on what you are doing, your community will stay with you.

Josh Maag is the founder of **SquareHook**, a drag and drop website-building tool. He wants to make it easy for beginners to use his tool to create good looking and well-functioning websites without knowing how to code. He hosts a meetup that is a 10 week website-building course both to introduce people to his product and to stay connected with his community of customers.

One of Pieter Levels' many startups is **Nomad List**. This site provides information for "digital nomads:" entrepreneurs and freelancers who travel the world and work from their laptops. One of the biggest draws of his site is **#nomads**, a chat group that allows digital nomads from all over the world to connect based on location or skillsets and talk about everything from where to find the best places to work, how to stay productive, and what equipment they are using.

How to start a club

Though the process for starting a club can vary from university to university, most clubs work with the student government, and often have a very simple application process. Here are some of the most common steps:

- Make sure the club does not exist already - the university won't support two of the same club, so if your club idea already exists you have two options:

- Find a way to differentiate your club from what already exists
- Join the current club and work to take on a leadership role

- Define the purpose of your club - It's best to focus the club around a single idea. This helps people identify with the club and to decide if it is right for them. Often the purpose of your club will need to be written in a "club constitution." Make sure you constitution does not conflict with the mission of your student government or university as a whole.

- Register with the student government - This is usually a one-page paper and if you have done your homework on what clubs exist already, it should be very easy. Also keep in mind you will likely have to register your club every year.

- Promote your club - To start promoting your club, it's best to host a launch event with a specific date and rather than just announcing weekly meetings. Consider having an interesting speaker, or some other kind of engaging activity to build buzz. Here's a few ideas for promotion:

  - Post flyers (with permission) around your university
  - Reach out to your school newspaper
  - Visit classes with subject related to your club
  - Get local businesses to sponsor the event
  - Get your university's marketing office to post the event on social media
  - Get the event shared on your university's event calendar
  - Don't just promote to students, try to get faculty and administration interested
  - Contact your alumni association and promote the event to alumni

Expand your club with meetups

You may be able to expand the reach of your club off-campus by creating a meetup. Meetup is a website that helps facilitate communities in cities across the world. It's very easy to start a meetup and most cities have thousands of active members.

Why have a meetup?

Creating a meetup for your club will attract people who are interested in your idea but aren't directly connected with your university. Having a meetup in place will also empower you to keep your community alive after your graduate.

Not only will a meetup attract more people but it can attract members of the professional community to your idea as well. Depending on the core idea of your club, this could add value in many ways.

- Club sponsors - If a local business resonates with your club you may be able to attract a sponsor. Having the club open to people off campus could attract employees that advocate for sponsoring the club.
- Diversify ideas - Having members from the professional community can bring new ideas to your club and add value to your meetings and events.
- Build connections - The connections you make with the people in your club may lead to relationships that help build your business.

In the next chapter I'll give you a framework for a club that you can start for entrepreneurs. It is a model that is being used around the world and has transformed hundreds of students into successful entrepreneurs.

If you want to learn more about the power of tribes and strategies for build communities around ideas, check out Tribes: **We Need You to Lead Us,** by Seth Godin.

Key Takeaways

- A thriving club or meetup establishes you as an authority and a leader.
- Use your university to help you get momentum and build on that by reaching out to your community.
- Attach your club to your personal brand to build momentum for your work.
- Combine your club with a meetup and get people from off-campus to attend and participate.
- Use university funding to invite interesting speakers and put together events that build your brand and grow the club.

Chapter 16

THE FOUNDRY - THE SECRET RECIPE FOR ENTREPRENEURSHIP

At the Foundry, I made close friends that continue to amaze and inspire me. Here's the story of one of them.

Cassidy was a young snowboarder from Idaho. He was a skilled craftsman and designer; he could build tiny houses, sew clothing and design websites and graphics. But he was also quite shy and unsure of himself.

The first day of the foundry, Cassidy found himself in a room of 30 people. He was so paralyzed with shyness that he did not introduce himself to anyone at the first meeting.

He joined the Foundry to build a print shop with his girlfriend. They set up their large printer and supplies in the coworking space where the Foundry met. His girlfriend handled the marketing and sales, while he did the fulfillment and design. For him, the thought of speaking in front of a group or calling a customer to close a sale was terrifying.

After a few months he separated with his girlfriend, leaving him homeless, carless, and business-partnerless, sleeping in the cubicle he had built in the coworking space. He had no money saved, and only the choice to return to his home or make his business work. He slept on the floor each night underneath his desk, and cooked most of his meals out of a small rice-cooker. Without the help of his girlfriend, sales started to slow down and money became very tight.

Cassidy continued to participate in the weekly meetings, and built relationships with the entrepreneurs who worked in the coworking space. The friends and connections he made helped him overcome his fears and recover his business and his life.

He took a job as a pedicabber (a mix between a bike and a taxi), working nights to bring in extra cash. Hustling prints by day and pedestrians by night. With the support of the community of entrepreneurs he met though the Foundry, he kept working hard despite the impossibly difficult situation he faced. He learned how to speak with customers, close a sale, and promote his business. He sharpened his sales skills further night-by-night through pedicabbing.

Barely a year later, Cassidy was in front of a large group of entrepreneurs giving a presentation on his business, explaining his target market, how he worked with his customers, and some of the challenges he faced. He was charismatic and energetic. Cassidy found an apartment he could afford with the earnings from his business. Within a year of joining the Foundry, Cassidy had reinvented himself.

Cassidy wanted to travel and inspire others to follow their dreams through photography. He had ambitions to bike through New Zealand, Australia, and Southeast Asia. Hauling people on a Pedicab night-by-night had strengthened him for the challenge. The months he spent living in a cubicle taught him to live simply and he was quickly able to save for his journey. Using the sales skills he developed with his print business, he found sponsors and began to build interest in his new project.

Today Cassidy is in New Zealand traveling around the country practicing photography and taking design jobs online and odd jobs on the road to finance his adventure. He found the confidence and the skills to control the direction of his life, and to follow his passions and dreams. He learned to be open to the kindness of others and to have the confidence to put himself in uncertain situations.

Although it is far from a six figure business or a billion dollar exit, Cassidy found his own definition of entrepreneurship. Cassidy discovered what he loved to do, and found his own way to do it.

What is the Foundry?

Entrepreneurship can be a very lonely endeavor. You take on the responsibility of solving new and increasingly challenging problems every day. It takes courage to believe in what you are doing and to have faith in simple beginnings. Most of your friends or family probably won't understand what you are doing or why you are doing it.

The Foundry is a community for aspiring entrepreneurs. The foundry is a place where you can go to be understood and to get help solving problems. It is a place for "doers," people who were committed to building a business and taking small steps each week to make it a reality. The goal of the Foundry is not to create a business, but to create an entrepreneur. With my group, we celebrated failures as much as successes; we recognized failure as an integral part of building a business and knew that if you weren't failing sometimes, you were missing something.

There were three main components to the Foundry, all relatively simple ideas that combined led to powerful results. The Foundry consisted of weekly meetings to solve problems, social events to build relationships, and project reviews to make sure we were on the right track.

Monday morning meetings

The Foundry would meet once a week to discuss achievements and problems from the past week and goals for the coming week. We used simple documents to track and share progress, these documents were shared with the group.

Over the weekend we would share an update with the group, telling people about our progress for the week, and about our hangups. Everyone would review the group's updates and brainstorm ways to help solve someone's problem or to provide support.

The problems that we were not able to solve over the weekend were brought up for discussion in the morning meeting. Though none of us were gurus or startup wizards, we relied on the power of 20 minds set on solving a problem. There was bound to be someone who knew what next step to take, or knew someone who was an expert and who we could invite to come speak to us about the issue.

Social events

At the first meeting the director asked for volunteers to help coordinate social events for the Foundry. Every Wednesday evening we would set up a dinner, or invite a speaker to come and discuss a topic. I volunteered to be the coordinator; it seemed like a perfect opportunity to build relationships with interesting people, and a way to have them help answer my questions.

Before joining the Foundry, it was easy for me to reach out to local businesses and entrepreneurs around the country and simply say "Hi I'm a student and I would like to ask you about…" but now I had even more opportunity with "Hi, I have a group of 20 students who are all starting businesses and want to invite you to speak about…"

We had discussions on marketing, 3d printing, taxes, hiring, design, building a website and more. If the person we wanted to talk with was not local, they would often agree to do a Skype call with us.

Project reviews

Once a month, each student entrepreneur would schedule a project review.

In the same way CEO's of large companies have board members, the student would invite mentors, peers, and sometimes clients to discuss the progress of their business and to set new goals. The student was responsible for making the arrangements for their project review and for getting the right people to attend.

They would present their progress in a brief slideshow and field questions from their board. Their board was expected to be highly critical and honest. It was not always an easy experience, but the process would give the student valuable insights into their business and direction for the future.

Origins of the Foundry

The Foundry started with a professor with a pizza budget and a small group of students who wanted to start businesses. They committed to helping each other face the challenges and solve the problems of starting a business.

These weren't the typical "top of the class" kind of students either. They were awkward, rebellious, unassuming students who had yet to find their way.

They met once a week to discuss their progress and their problems with the businesses they were starting. The committed to making progress on their business every week, and prioritized helping others in the group over helping themselves. They held each other accountable and supported each other through challenges and uncertainty.

This small community of mostly undergraduate students was at first dismissed by most of campus. Nobody thought undergraduates could start businesses; everyone thought they would need more experience or knowledge before they could be successful.

But as some of the businesses these students were growing began to generate six figure revenues they started to get more attention. These students proved that it was possible for anyone to start a business.

As the students transformed into entrepreneurs, the Foundry grew into an integral part of the entrepreneurship program at the University of Utah.

Some of these students dropped out to continue to grow their businesses. Others went on to be consultants and helped large businesses implement the same strategies and ideas they used in their businesses. Some went on to create foundries across the world to help spread the ideas and the systems that helped them grow into entrepreneurship.

How to start your own foundry

Creating your own foundry is easier than you might expect, and it is the perfect environment in which to put most of the tactics I have outlined in this book to the test. Instead of trying to hack your university and build a business on your own, why not have a group of students pooling their resources to connect with interesting people, to build successful businesses and to become entrepreneurs.

The goal of the foundry is not necessarily to create successful businesses, but to create entrepreneurs with the skills to build businesses. Instead of focusing on the success of a business, it focuses on education and to developing the mindset that leads to the long-term success of an entrepreneur. A failed business is not the end of an entrepreneur; it's a victory. The foundry is a place where failures can be celebrated and shared as sources of knowledge.

With a few simple documents, you can run your own Foundry. You can download your own set of documents to create a Foundry at your school at Kylegray.io/resources.

Action steps to start your own foundry

Start a club - It's easy to start a club at universities. You univeristy will probably provide funding for meetings and events, and may be able to help you find a location to host meeting and events. Take advantage of university resources so you can buy some pizza for people who show up, and create some flyers or other marketing material to get the word out across campus.

Get the word out - Look around campus for other students who are interested in starting businesses. Though the business school is an obvious place to start, you can find the entrepreneurial spirit in many different students across campus. It's best to have a diverse group of talents and perspectives so find artists, programmers, engineers, linguists, internationalists.

What to look for in members:

- **Passion**: The failure or success of the Foundry depends on the energy and passion the team brings to the table. The team needs to have a passion not only for business, but for learning from and teaching others.

- **Coachability**: People need to be open to receiving feedback from others. This can mean being open to both praise and criticism. You may be able to have experts come speak to your group but the most important feedback will come from your peers who show up every week. They need to have an open mind and be willing to wrestle with uncomfortable ideas and situations.

An environment where everyone is coachable means that everyone can show up to weekly meetings fully prepared to be vulnerable and to share both their successes and their struggles.

- **Diligence**: You don't need to spend 80 hours each week trying to build your business, but you do need to be diligent in taking small steps each week to move toward your goals. Look for people who can stay focused and motivated. Even when things are difficult and uncertain they will keep showing up with the best they have to offer.

- **Risk taking**: You want people who are ready to make a bet on themselves and take risks for the sake of their business. This could mean being willing to pay for an expensive conference for the chance to meet potential customers. Or to invest in making a great video for a crowdfunding campaign while still feeling fear that nobody will like their product.

You need people who are willing to experiment, to make mistakes and to fail. Nobody has ever been successful without leaving a trail of failures behind them. The best people will be willing to fail, be open to learning from their failures, and to sharing the lessons they learned in the process.

Keep in mind the Foundry process is set up not to create businesses, but to create entrepreneurs. A failed (or successful) business is just one step on the path of the entrepreneur.

Commit for at least 12 weeks - Once you have your group, commit to 12 weeks or more of meeting every week and taking small steps toward starting a business. Choose a time that works for the whole group (or as many members as possible).

For us this was typically Monday morning at 7:00am. The meeting concluded before most classes or jobs started, and the meeting was a good way to start the week off with some positive motivation.

Commit to showing up each week to help others; don't be concerned about yourself. If you focus on helping others get their businesses working then you will benefit as well.

The foundry culture

A key part of the foundry culture was that every member was treated like the CEO of a large company. This meant that there was little tolerance for those showing up late or not participating in the process. Each member was expected to be fiercely committed to helping the group, not just themselves.

This strict nature was meant to build trust between the members. Starting a business can be very stressful and scary, and with this disciplined culture the members felt safe to be vulnerable with the group and share what they were struggling with.

It felt strange at first to expect such discipline from a group of young students. But simply by setting these expectations the behavior of the students changed. They started to act like CEO's, not only in the meetings but during the week. Some students won't be prepared for this commitment and may leave; this is a good thing. The ones that stay will form tight bonds and help each other achieve incredible things.

Hosting weekly meetings

These meetings are the core of the Foundry. Each week, your group should show up prepared for an hour of highly concentrated problem solving. Everyone should be prepared to provide whatever assistance they can to the group.

There are two ways these meetings can be conducted.

Free-for-all - If you have a large group, a free-for-all where people can present problems they have been facing and share progress may be ideal. Not everyone is required to talk.

Hot seat - For a smaller group, consider having a rotating hot seat where one person will present a challenge they are facing for 10 minutes, then have the entire group ask questions and provide feedback on the challenge for 30 minutes. The hot seat will rotate between members each week so everyone gets a chance to have their problems worked on.

Hold each other accountable - We used a document called a Management Report to record and share our progress and problems each week and to make plans for the following week. We would share all of these documents in a shared google drive folder three days before our meeting. Everyone would review the documents, leave comments, and try to solve the problems that members of the group were facing.

At each meeting if someone was facing a challenge they could bring it up to the group. With the collective knowledge and the network of the group, there was almost never a problem that we could not solve. If we all shared a challenge or ran into something we could not solve, we usually had a connection with someone who could help teach us.

Planning social events

Each week you should have a social event. These events are a way for the group to bond and get to know each other personally since the weekly meetings wills be mostly focused on business and progress. Social events can be fun or an opportunity to invite an expert to speak on a topic that the group is interested in.

You may want to find someone else in the cohort who will be in charge of planning these events. This will help divide responsibilities and give others some ownership in the group. Though one person should be responsible for making these events happen, the whole group should feel like they have a part making these events successful.

Here's a few ideas for weekly events:

Workshops: Perhaps there is a common topic that you are all struggling with, such as social media marketing. See if there is someone on the team who would be willing to learn as much as they can about the topic in a week or two and put on a presentation for the group.

They could purchase an online course from somewhere like **Digital Marketer** (most of their courses include certifications too). Perhaps you could use some of the club's budget from the university to help pay for the course, or split the cost between the group.

After a week or two of intensive learning, have that individual put on a 30-45 minutes presentation on the topic sharing the highlights of their learnings with the group.

Consider recording these workshops as well and encourage the presenters to post them on their personal websites.

Invite interesting people: If you are facing a common challenge or have a common interest in your group, see if there is a person in your city or online who has solved the problem. Reaching out to someone as a group of 20 students leverages and multiplies the same "student title" power mentioned earlier in the book. So it's likely you'll be able to get higher profile people to agree to speak.

If you want to reach out to someone who's not in your city, consider doing a live **Hangout on Air** so the talk can be recorded and shared with others who want to learn the same topics. The person you interview may also share the talk with their audience and get some additional exposure for your businesses.

Launch parties: If someone in the group is launching a product on **Kickstarter** or releasing a new ebook on Amazon, consider hosting a launch party. If you have a club registered with your university it may be possible to get a large room, food, and marketing assistance from your university.

Have everyone in the cohort work together to invite as many of their friends as possible. Give the person who is launching a chance to make a speech during the party and talk about their product to build enthusiasm and awareness.

If possible, find a place where you could have several laptops or tables set up so people who are attending the party can contribute to the crowdfunding campaign or download the book while at the party.

Better with friends

Entrepreneurship is a team sport. The Foundry process is about creating a team who help educate each other and assist each other through the process of becoming entrepreneurs. It's a challenging and often lonely process; having a group of people who are facing these challenges in lockstep helps you learn the critical skills for starting a business faster.

You will attract other students who are interested in building a business, taking control of their lives, and finding clever solutions to problems. As a group you'll have more influence with professors, administration, and thought leaders than you would have on your own. Many new opportunities may present themselves to you. You'll create a tribe of close friends who will understand you in ways most people won't. You will build long-term relationships that will unfold in ways you can't currently imagine.

Key Takeaways

- Entrepreneurship can be lonely. Having a group to support you makes the process easier.
- The goal of the foundry is not to create successful businesses, but to create entrepreneurs with the skills to build businesses.
- Meet once a week to report progress and help solve problems, to accelerate the results of your business and to keep you accountable.
- Working hard side-by-side with other entrepreneurs will forge some of the strongest friendships and relationships in your life.
- Use social events to connect with other entrepreneurs and to help your cohort bond with each other.

PART 4

Expanding your influence off-campus

Chapter 17

THE SECRET WEAPON OF STUDENTS

I have always loved skiing. I grew up in the mountains and my father is a ski patroller, so I learned to appreciate skiing from a very young age.

It is a culture and industry that I understand and am passionate about. So I wanted my business to set me up in some way to engage with the outdoor industry. In my hometown there were dozens if not hundreds of businesses in the outdoor industry. I knew that many of them might need help with marketing online, the service my business was providing. But I imagined they were constantly bombarded with emails, calls and other solicitations from marketers. Why would they trust me over anyone else? I had little to no experience and I was not even sure if what I was offering was something they needed.

I decided I at least needed to figure out if they wanted my service. To do that I needed to talk with the owners and learn about their problems. But how was I going to get the attention of these businesses when there were likely hundreds of other marketers who would love to get this same information from them?

It turns out I had one of the most powerful tools at my disposal. Not only were they willing to talk, but they offered to take me out to lunch, give me tours of their businesses, and share details about their business that I'm sure few others were privy to.

My secret weapon was that I was a student. I would look up local businesses I was interested in working with and either call or email them something along the lines of:

"Hello,
My name is Kyle, I'm a student at the University of Utah and I am doing research
on online marketing and conversion optimization. I was wondering if I could

talk to you about some of the problems your business is facing for a project I am working on..."

The person on the other end was almost always floored; they rarely heard from students and never heard from students who were trying to solve their problems. They often responded with enthusiasm and openness to my request. It was easy to arrange lunch meetings or a tour of their headquarters where they would introduce me to everyone on their team.

No other marketers were having success like this on their cold calls.

The student card

One of the biggest advantages you have as a student is the title. Simply declaring "I'm a student" in the right situations can open more doors than the degree you earn when you graduate. You can use your student status at a tool for networking and building connections that will help your business.

Being a student is revered and respected position in American culture and in many places around the world. Many people are happy to help students with their education if given the opportunity. This effect is especially powerful with emerging entrepreneurs and authors who have a niche following but are not yet household names.

Most students at some point are offered a seat at the dinner table or a couch to sleep on from friends and family. But most people never their status as a student to build new connections and open new doors. They stay on campus for their entire education and do very little to put what they are learning into practice. But this is good news for you, because you now know that you possess a secret weapon to build the knowledge and network necessary for a thriving business.

Just the other day a student from Switzerland reached out to me for help on her thesis paper about "marketing for startups" I was thrilled to get the email and happy to make time to help her out. Even though there was a big difference between our time zones, I was willing to move my schedule around to accommodate her because it felt good to have a student ask my opinion on things.

Consider how you can use this to grow your business.

Create reasons to reach out

Perhaps you thinking "I'm not a business student, I don't take any classes that would give me an excuse to reach out to them."

Even if you don't have a way to directly tie this to your schoolwork, just the fact that you are a student will open people up to talking with you. I encourage you to try it out a few times before you use it for schoolwork just to see what will happen.

In previous chapters we've discussed creating customized majors and course-work to take your education into your own hands. Having the freedom to create coursework that would reward you for making connections is one of the main reasons custom majors or directed readings are so valuable. You're killing two birds with one stone: earning credit towards graduation and building a network so that once you graduate you'll be miles ahead of the pack.

You don't necessarily have to be doing these projects for credit. We've also talked about starting clubs and meetups on or off campus. If you don't have a way to connect it to your coursework, then reach out on behalf of your club.

Invite people out to lunch

As a student you should aim to have lunch at least once a week with someone you want to connect with. Invite that person who lives in your city and has a similar business or does similar work to what you want to do for your business.

It can be intimidating to approach a superior and ask them for their time like this. So start by giving them an ego boost with some admiration. Let them know you are a student and want to follow in their footsteps and learn how to be like them. Then ask them out to lunch to talk about it. This will fill them with a sense of pride, and give them some nostalgic pleasure. Almost everyone wishes they could go back in time and give advice to themselves when they were 18. In many ways you are giving them this opportunity.

Offer to pay for lunch since they are taking time to meet with you (it's well worth the investment), but it's likely they'll insist on paying for yours.

You'll be surprised at how open people are to meeting with students. It may take some practice to figure out the best ways to contact and interact with the people you want to work with. So don't be discouraged if it does not work on your first try. If possible, it should be a weekly ritual of yours to meet with someone over lunch and to learn from them. You have time to perfect your methods and will grow more comfortable in approaching people.

Here's a few sample questions you could ask them.

- What do they like about their work?
- What do they not like?
- How did they get started doing what they are doing now?
- What would they have done differently if they could start over?

- What problems are they having?
- What strategies or processes could make their work better?

Each of these little questions helps you better paint a picture of your future business and the work you want to do. You will begin to have a much better understanding of what the job is like and about the problems that need to be solved. This knowledge will make you much more competitive in your business, even if in the future you won't be working directly with the people you lunch with.

After a few months of weekly lunches, you'll be surprised at how quickly you can grow your network and you'll start to see new and interesting opportunities appear as more people get to know you.

Visit the a business or potential client

Do you want to visit a local business to see what it would be like to work with them? Maybe you would like to help people in a similar way and want to know how they do it. Call them up and say you're a student doing research and would like to check out how they run things.

Develop a theme of questions that might help you understand the business, how it works with its customers and its problems. Or if they serve a similar customer to your target customer, try to learn how you could apply what they are doing well to your own business. Here are's some good areas to ask about:

What are their strengths/advantages? - You can't be the best at everything. Most businesses choose to focus on doing a few things very well and differentiate themselves based on that. You'll need to find your own set of unique advantages for your business, and understanding what others are focusing on will help guide this process.

- Marketing - Have they mastered certain marketing channels to drive customer interest?
- Customer service - How do they make their customers happy? How do they interact with the customer? What do they do that causes customers to talk to their friends about the business?
- Price - Are they able to deliver lower prices than anyone else? How can they do this? Are they able to charge much more than anyone else?
- Team - Do they have a talented and motivated team? Why do people like working there? Did the team members have history with the business before they started working there?

What are their bottlenecks for growth? What is keeping this business from doubling in size?

- Do people know about them?
- Is there too much work for too few team members?
- Are they targeting the wrong customers?

What are the company's values? Understanding the values of a business will help you understand their competitive advantage and what the goals of the business are. If the values resonate with you, see how you could apply them to your own work. If they don't, figure out how you would do things differently.

Write short research papers related to your business

What are some of the main problems that your customers or businesses like yours face? Understanding the problems your customers or competitors face will give you a glimpse into the potential opportunities and pitfalls of your business.

Consider writing a paper based on one of these problems and offer a plan for a solution. Reach out to leaders in your areas of interest and ask them about these problems.

After speaking with a few people, do some research to investigate how others have solved this problem before. Be aware of what resources (team members, time, money) the people you interviewed had available, and propose a solution based on examples you have discovered.

Come up with an action plan that they could implement to solve the problem. If possible cite examples of how others have overcome similar obstacles. Once you're finished, share the paper with the people you interviewed and ask them to let you know if they applied your advice to their business.

You may not think that you have the knowledge or experience to solve this problem. But as a young student you have something very valuable to offer the world. You have time, energy and willingness to learn. Many of the problems people face exist simply because they currently don't have the time or energy to direct to solving them. Taking some of your time to research and create a strategy to solve a problem might make all the difference.

If the strategy you propose works, then you've got a bonafide product or service to offer others.

Turn your meetings and research into content

Don't keep the insights you get from these meetings to yourself. Create content for your personal blog that shares what you have learned. Make sure you get permission if you are sharing specific details about a business or person.

People will be interested in what you are learning. If you are meeting people that relate to the business you want to start, it's likely that creating content about them will be interesting to potential customers or other businesses that you could work with in the future.

Even if you are trying to solve a problem for a business, make sure you portray them in a positive light. Make the content you create something they would be interested in sharing.

Keep in touch

Once you establish these connections make sure you nurture them. Your title of "student" will only get you through the door. From there is up to you to use your magic to find ways to move the relationship forward. If you find people that resonate with you and what you want to create, then this should be easy. Don't be afraid of doing free work if you need to get some experience or a good recommendation.

So keep in touch with the people you meet through this process, stay up to date on changes in their businesses or lives, and keep them posted on the progress you are making.

Key Takeaways

- Your title of "student" is one of the most power powerful tools you have to build relationships.
- Create reasons to reach out to local businesses, thought leaders, and other people you are interested in speaking with.
- Find opportunities to solve their problems,building your skills and reputation in the process.
- Take the lessons that your learn and turn them into content for your personal brand.

Chapter 18

HOW AND WHY TO INVITE SOMEONE TO SPEAK AT YOUR UNIVERSITY

One of my favorite writers during my time at university was **Mark Manson**. His articles on happiness, relationships, and finding purpose in life deeply resonated with me. I would eagerly await fresh articles each week on his blog.

He was also one of the first people to give me a different perspective on what a "business" was or could look like. He was traveling the world, living in dozens of different countries while making a living off books and courses he has created. He broke down how he did this in an article called "**How To Quit Your Day Job And Travel The World**".

That was a world I desperately wanted to understand. Travel had been a big source of personal growth for me and I was perpetually seeking out new opportunities to travel. While I had some small experience building websites I didn't have the skillset to do what Mark was doing yet.

An opportunity to connect with Mark finally appeared. Mark posted that he was looking for speaking opportunities across the US and was open to speaking with small or large groups. I wrote him and asked if he would be interested in coming out to Utah. He said he would be and gave me a price for what it would cost to have him speak.

I scheduled a meeting with the events coordinator for the student government at my university. I was not sure if they were going to be open to this request or not; I figured the budget for speakers and events for the year might have already been used up.

I had a short pitch prepared, explaining who Mark was, what he wrote about, and why I wanted him to come speak. Finally, I was asked how much he would charge to come speak. I was nervous about this part; I had never asked for money before for something like this. Though I was afraid, I didn't hesitate and told him what it would cost to have Mark come speak.

That's when something unbelievable happened. He responded with a calm "yes" and asked if I wanted the student government's help promoting the event. We coordinated when the event would take place and where a good venue on campus would be.

I was blown away… A few weeks earlier I had worked for hours to apply for a scholarship for about the same amount of money. I had to compete with hundreds of other students to make my application stand out. Meanwhile, with a brief conversation I got funding to fly out a hero of mine and help him put together an awesome event.

Fast forward a few months, and Mark was in town. Flyers were all over campus promoting the event and stacks of hot pizza were delivered to lure in hungry students. The room was completely full; all the chairs were taken and people were crowding in the back.

Best of all, I was asked to introduce Mark to the group. I got up in front of the room and gave him a brief but energetic introduction. As I looked out over the room I could hardly believe that this was a reality. My university gave me money to meet someone I admired and wanted to learn from, and gave me the opportunity to do him a huge favor in securing this speaking gig for him.

Mark simply had to plug in his laptop and open up his presentation and speak. It was an easy win for him.

After the event I had the chance to go out to dinner with Mark. I took him to one of my favorite Thai food restaurants and showed him one of Salt Lake's local breweries. We talked about different places we had traveled, and I asked him some of the burning questions I had about starting a business and living like he did.

After dinner we went to a BBQ my friend was hosting; I introduced Mark to my friends and he fit right in. Before, I had imagined him as some sort of genius, born with a brilliant mind that could easily create great writing and build a lifestyle around it. But that was far from the truth. Mark, though a little older than me, was just a regular guy. He was easy to relate to, he laughed at the same jokes, and blended right in with my group of friends.

This personal experience with Mark made my own goals seem much more achievable. He was not a super-human, but he found a way to live life on his terms. If he could do it, I could do the same.

Who should you invite to speak?

Inviting someone to speak at your university is a quick way to bridge the gap between you and someone you look up to. And, this is a two-way street; being invited to speak at a university or in front of a group of students is a very flattering experience. There are many ways this speaking event can unfold into a valuable relationship.

Though this is possible to reach out to big celebrities, they'll require more work and money to book and your request will feel like less of a favor to them. I recommend aiming smaller. Look for people who are locally renowned in your city or are rising stars online. Another good rule of thumb would be to think of someone who you would like to be like in 5-10 years and who might be able to help you advance your business in the future.

Here's a few people to consider:

- Local business owners - The founder of a local ski/surf/skate company that you like.
- Emerging authors - Someone who is independently published, maybe

has one or two books out.

- Bloggers, podcasters, Youtube celebrities - People with growing audiences on new media are usually thrilled to get a chance to speak at a university.
- Activists - People who are committed to a cause that resonates with you.

How you can invite them to speak

Universities have thousands of dollars each semester budgeted for speakers. Every year the student government and administration desperately try to come up with ideas for events and speakers. The funds are often underused or the events that they plan are under-attended.

Rarely does a student come forward with an idea for someone to speak. This leaves the administration trying to guess at what would make a good event. They want to hear from you. If you bring an idea forward, there is a very high chance that they will help you make it happen.

Here are a few ways your university can help:

- Funding to pay the speaker
- Reserving a venue on or off campus for the event
- Marketing for the event on campus
- Pizza or other catering to bribe hungry students to attend

Step one: Find a speaker

Choose someone with previous speaking experience and with ideas related to your interests. Do some work to build a relationship with them and start a dialogue. After you have some report developed, ask if they would be interested in speaking at your university. If they seem open to the idea, it's time to find a place to host the event.

You'll want to consider what the person you invite will be speaking about. This will help you decide where to go to pitch the idea.

For topics that would apply to the student population at large you can approach your student government. This is a great option; they usually have the largest budgets and staff to help you promote the event.

If it is a topic that would apply to a certain field of study, try approaching a college or department that discusses similar topics. Also look for power centers, offices and organizations that are high-profile and well-funded at your university.

Active clubs on campus can also be influential partners. They won't have as many disposable funds, but this is not necessarily a bad thing. You may not be able to make a huge event with a club, but a smaller event with an intensely interested, engaged audience can be just as impactful and memorable for a speaker as a crowded room. Or the club can help demonstrate interest for the event and influence the student government to support your idea.

Step two: Test the waters

Find the person responsible for coordinating events or marketing in the venue you want to work with. Ask to set up an in-person meeting with them to discuss having your speaker come.

When you go to the meeting have a basic outline of the speaker's background and what you want them to talk about. You'll want to figure out what the process is like for coordinating an event like this. Here are some basic things you should ask about and understand:

- How much time in advance is needed for an event like this (the bigger

the event, the longer)?
- What rooms are available?
- What amenities for speakers are available (audio / visual equipment, a hotel on campus if the speaker is not local)?
- What kind of marketing is available for the event?
- Catering for the event (pizza and soda is usually all you need)

At the same time you'll want to be working with your prospective speaker on the idea as well. You'll want to figure out a few pieces of information from them:

- What would they charge to speak (including travel, lodging, meals)?
- When would they be available to come to your university?
- Do they have any new topics they want to speak about?

You may not have all the information that either party wants in the beginning, but once a tentative date and budget are set then the hardest part is over.

Step three: Promote the event

You'll want to start promoting the event around campus. You'll have some help from the office you are working with, but you want to make sure that the event is as full as possible.

Create a facebook event with all of the details, so it is easy for people to share once they get the link.

I also recommend creating a simple email template with details about the event that people can copy and paste and send out effortlessly. Send this to different people across campus to build awareness.

Here's a few ideas for people to reach out to:

- **Professors** - If the speaker is related to something they teach about or are interested in, they'll not only be happy to mention it to their classes, but may even create some "extra credit" work or a small required assignment based on the event.
- **Academic advisors** - If the speaker's topic is somehow related to the college, advisors can help promote the event by giving flyers out in their office, telling students about it, and they usually have email lists of all of the students in the college.
- **University marketing** - Universities usually have a marketing office that controls all of their social media accounts. These accounts usually have thousands of followers. The marketing offices are always looking for new events to promote on campus.
- **University media** - Many universities have student-run newspapers and radio stations that may be interested in helping you promote your event.
- **Clubs and meetups** - If you can relate what the speaker is talking about to a local club or meetup they may work with you to promote it.
- **Fraternities or sororities** - Every fraternity and sorority has a history and values they try to embody. If you can relate your speaker's topic to one of these traits, you may be able to get a large group of students from here.
- **Student affairs offices** - Places like the international student center, veteran's support, diversity center, all cater to different types of students and are usually happy to promote an event that might be interesting to their community.

If you are in a city with multiple universities or colleges in the area, consider reaching out to these groups in other universities and drawing their students to your event as well.

Step Four: When the speaker comes to the university

This is really your time to shine. If the speaker is flying into town, offer to pick them up from the airport.
Help them with basic logistics. Will they need audio equipment or a screen for their presentation? Do they have flyers or information they need to print out? Do they know their way around campus?

Be prepared to introduce the speaker. Give a brief, enthusiastic introduction and let the speaker do the rest.

After the event, invite the speaker out to dinner. If they aren't local, take some time to show them around town a little bit. Feel free to invite anyone that might be a good person for the speaker to meet. Help them make connections with people who may be valuable to them.

If all goes well you should have a solid new connection that will help you on your path to your business or brand.
Use this as an opportunity for speaking practice

You'll develop an incredible network and reputation by connecting thought leaders with your campus. With each successful event it will become easier to have higher-profile speakers and more interesting conversations.

As you become more comfortable with hosting these events, consider creating a short talk or presentation that you could use to open for the speakers you invite. This will position you as an authority and thought leader in your own right. This could lead to more speaking gigs for yourself in the future.

Key takeaways

- Universities have large budgets for speakers each year.
- Student rarely propose ideas for events; you can use this to get interesting people on campus.
- Most people are honored to speak at universities and they'll be grateful to you for giving them the opportunity.
- Take the opportunity to show the speaker around your city and get to know them personally.
- Use these events as an opportunity to practice your own speaking skills: make a short introduction or try out a short talk of your own.

Chapter 19

HOW TO GET A PERFECT LETTER OF RECOMMENDATION

I had just finished my first project with my first client. I had run a few tests on their website to find ways to make it easier for the visitor to use and purchase their product. I got some good results on a page and boosted how many people were clicking on a "shop now" button. I had worked hard to find ways to improve their website and discovered that it was equally important to explain what I was doing to their team and get their support.

Since this was the first business that let me near their website I didn't charge anything. What was important was the experience I gained, and a testimonial from the founder who had originally invited me to run this experiment with their website. I needed this testimonial to be amazing; it had to convince future customers to work with me and pay for my services.

The founder, Scott Paul, was a busy man: he had a large team and business was in the early stages of being acquired by another company. Though he liked me, I knew it would be difficult to get a good testimonial from him. I also knew that he was not watching every move I made. Nor did he know all the details of my work, so it seemed unfair to him to ask him to write this kiiler testimonial all by himself, to ask him to figure out what impression I wanted to make on future clients.

"So why not help him out?" I thought to myself.

I sat down and wrote what I thought would be the best possible testimonial for my work. I wanted to communicate the results I got, but also some of my soft skills.

Once it was ready, I sent him an email thanking him for the opportunity and complementing the team he had built. I let him know I was looking for a testimonial for my work but acknowledged that he was very busy. I told him that I had taken some time to help him out and had written a draft of the testimonial for him. He could use it as is, or modify it however he wanted. I mentioned I would also send a recommendation request via Linkedin as soon as I had his permission.

Here was the testimonial:

"It was a pleasure working with Kyle on improving the usability and conversion rates on our websites. He has a unique and creative perspective and a strong sense of customer empathy that gets results. He helped us improve email opt-ins by 145% on one of our sites. He is well organized and easy to communicate with, he developed lasting friendships while collaborating with our team and left a meaningful contribution to our company."

Scott was not only thrilled that I had saved him time. But was impressed with my approach. I was applying some of the same principles I used to encourage people to take action on his site to make it easy for him to take action and help me out.

Within a few hours the testimonial was up on my Linkedin profile, unchanged from my draft.

When to use recommendations?

If you are planning to use the tactics in this book, you'll probably run into some resistance from professors and administrators at your university. It's uncommon to encounter students who want to create custom coursework, custom internships, or start a business before they graduate; people may not know how to react. A good recommendation from the right person can help things move forward. It builds trust and shows you're someone who can get results.

Recommendations are common for applying for scholarships, jobs, undergraduate research and internships. But they can be even more effective when they are not required as part of an application.

For example, if you would like to ask a professor to oversee custom coursework you have put together to research a problem businesses are facing, why not include a recommendation from one or several of the businesses you are working with to demonstrate how reliable you are?

How to craft the perfect recommendation

Recommendation letters are a tedious process for both parties. Let's consider the position of the recommender. If you ask someone to write a letter for you, you are asking them to take time not only to write out the letter but to think about:

- What you did for them
- How you added value to their lives
- How to frame it in a way that is relevant to what you are applying for or requesting
- What kind of impression their recommendation should make on the reader

This is a very time-consuming process and can be and a bit unpleasant. So you want to make this as easy as possible for your recommender.

Pick someone who trusts you and has seen you work. Think of someone who you have worked with or for before: a professor, a coworker, a boss, a mentor. Aim for someone who has worked with you on a project or job that involved skills that are relevant to what you need this recommendation for.

If possible, pick someone who knows the person you will be delivering the recommendation to and who is trusted by them. A recommendation from a personal connection holds much more weight.

Write out the requirements for the position or program you are applying for, and then rework them into traits about you. Be honest in choosing what to emphasize; you want to give a truthful representation of yourself.

You want your recommendation to reinforce how you are the perfect person to be selected:

- Scholarship applications - Scholarships usually look for a specific personality trait like "leadership" or experience.
- Job applications - Perfect for outlining the specific traits and experiences listed in the job posting.
- Custom coursework or internships - You'll need to frame yourself as someone who is very trustworthy, motivated, and independent. A recommendation can be evidence to support that.
- Linkedin recommendations - These are better if written not for a specific job, but to highlight your skills and accomplishments.
- Testimonials for a business - if you do freelance work of any kind, you can use this tactic to quickly collect great testimonials.

Frame it as part of a story

Humans are wired for storytelling. A good story taps into emotions and memory which can make a huge difference if your application is one of hundreds. Try to frame your recommendation as part of a bigger story.

- What hardships or challenges have you overcome?
- What's unique about you?
- What are you passionate about and how does it relate to the opportunity

you are applying for?

- How does the program you are applying for relate to a bigger story or goal?

Infuse these little bits of story into the recommendation and into your application at large.

Draft your recommendation letter

Draft a letter for your recommender. Write out specifics about what you did for them and what the results were. Do your best to connect each of you points with the program or position that you need the recommendation for. Its best if you use exact language from the job posting, description, or application materials.

Here's a sample from a job posting:

An ideal candidate will be able to:

- Take charge of a situation without needing micro-management or much supervision.

Here's how you could could speak to that in the recommendation:

"[your name] was incredibly helpful with [project], they took responsibility for the task and owned the situation without needing micro-management or much supervision"

Take the opportunity to write about your strengths and the skills you want to demonstrate.

A brief, concise recommendation is best. Try to keep it under 300 words.

Make sure the letter is completely ready to go. This includes having an email or mailing address in the letter so all your recommender has to do it copy and paste, or print and send.

Present the letter to the recommender

Send an email with the letter attached to your recommender. In your email, make sure to compliment your recommender and let them know how much a good recommendation will help you. Close the letter by asking for it to be submitted or returned to you be a certain date. I like giving them about three days; this urgent enough for them to make it a priority, but not so urgent that it is disruptive.

Consider a message like this:

Hello [Name],

I have been applying for [an amazing opportunity]. I was thinking of great people who know and trust me for recommendations and you immediately came to mind. This is a big opportunity for me, and a letter from you would make a big difference in my application.

I know you're busy, so I took the time to write out the letter for you. The letter is attached (or pasted below). Feel free to make any changes you wish, or to send it as is. I have included the details you need to send it. If possible please have this sent by [date]

Let me know if you have any questions,

Cheers,
[you]

Wait for confirmation and say thanks

Your recommender will usually respond quickly and almost never make any changes. Make sure to thank them for helping you, and keep them updated on your progress and whether or not you got what you were requesting.

Warning:

Never send these without permission. There's no faster way to destroy hard-earned trust with your recommender and to ruin your chances of getting what you are applying for than by creating a false recommendation.

Key Takeaways

- Recommenders can be very busy; make it as easy as possible for them to give you a great testimonial.
- Use exact language from the job posting or scholarship application in the recommendation you write for yourself.
- Frame your writing of your recommendation as a "time saver" for your recommender.
- Never send a recommendation you have written on behalf of someone else without their explicit permission.

Chapter 20

BUILD REAL WORLD SKILLS IN A CUSTOM INTERNSHIP

Jessica Malnik couldn't believe her luck. All her hard work has paid off in spades.

She was home from the University of Missouri for the summer and she wanted to make the most of the free time she had before she went back to school.

As a journalism student, she wanted to gain some practical experience working in her field. She had a bit of experience with social media marketing, and wanted to grow those skills. She reached out to a few newspapers and TV stations in her home town and asked if they had any internship positions available. She listed off her relevant skills and offered to work for free. She knew that the experience would pay off in the long run. She had to take a part-time job to earn money as well, but she saw a summer of hard work as a good investment.

One TV station was open to working with her, and with a few calls to an advisor back at Missouri she was earning credit for her internship.

She worked 20 hours a week managing the website and helping with social media for the TV station and made herself useful to as many people as possible at the station. She sought out opportunities to shadow and work with people at the station and built relationships along the way.

She returned to school with a new perspective, sharpened skills, and a good referral if she needed one.

Once she graduated, she checked back with the TV station to see if they had any paid positions open. They had an opening for a web producer, and she got the job with no problem. The job was not well-paid, but served as a springboard to work at an ad agency in New York, and as an online community manager for an ecommerce platform based in Austin, Texas.

She had been listening to a podcast for a few years called the **Tropical MBA**. She was inspired by the stories of entrepreneurs building businesses that would allow them to travel, facilitate their passions, and build wealth.

The podcast was part of a community called the **Dynamite Circle**. This community connected entrepreneurs, organized events and provided a forum where entrepreneurs would share information on how to grow businesses, about good places to travel and about ways to optimize their lifestyle.

Listening to the podcast one day, she heard they had a job opening for a community manager for the Dynamite Circle. Her past experience made her an ideal fit, and she landed a dream job working with a community of unique entrepreneurs.

Why should you do an internship?

You can only learn so much in a classroom, and without the perspective of working in a business or other organization it's hard to have direction in your education and to know what is valuable. The patterns and habits that we learn to help us succeed in a classroom are very different than those needed in the workplace. But with an understanding of what skills are valuable and competitive in the "real world," you'll be empowered to succeed in ways many new graduates aren't.

Most universities offer local and international internship opportunities. This is an excellent way to build skills and experience. An internship will give you the chance to work with an organization that tests your skills in the "real world." These organizations could be non-profits, government organizations, or large businesses.

Internship programs can give you access to very prestigious organizations and sometimes give you responsibility over important and interesting projects. Internships also give you a chance to "test the waters" and discover if the field you are interested in is really where you want to be. An internship that shows you what you don't want can give you the chance to change course before you invest years of your life developing skills for an industry you might end up hating.

Though there are many good options offered by internship programs, they are often very limited and may not closely relate to what you want to do.

Many internships programs are aware of this, and offer custom internships to intrepid students who want to seek out opportunities of their own. A custom internship is a way for you to try your hand in a field that interests you before you graduate. You can earn credit while honing the skills you are passionate about and you can influence what you study. Earning school credit while doing this can make you eligible for scholarships and other benefits.

How to setup a custom internship:

1 - Speak with the internship program at your university and ask if they offer custom internships.

Schedule an appointment with an advisor in the internship program. Sometimes internship programs are scattered throughout the university, and sometimes they are organized through one central office.

Share your plan to start a business and describe the skills you want to develop. The advisor can tell you about their current offerings. Ask if they also offer customized internship programs and what it would take to be approved one.

There are usually some basic requirements such as:

- Work with a legitimate, established organization
- Duties must be substantive, e.g. research, writing, meeting attendance, administrative assistance
- Host-office must have a dedicated work space
- Fulfills weekly hour requirements

These requirements are often very subjective. Which means you may be able to work around some of them if the plan you propose is not a perfect fit, as long as you make up for it in other areas.

Once you know that your university offers custom internships and understand what the requirements and limitations are for these programs, you can begin seeking out interesting places to work.

2 - Identify places where you would want to intern.

If you want to start your own business, I recommend finding a small business in your city that is similar to the kind of business you would like to start. Make a list of a few different businesses or organizations that interest you and see if you can find the contact information for the founder or the people in charge of the department you are interested in.

If it is a small business, it is unlikely that they have had an intern before. Small organizations are also likely to be short on resources, particularly time and focus. So approaching them point-blank with the request to do an internship will probably not work. Though you are offering free work, it will still require their time and thought to figure out how you can help them. So you need to figure out a way to fit in on your own.

Research what the company values, what makes it unique, and what projects it is working on.

Contact the business and mention you are a student working on a project and would like to know a little more about them. Let them know you are interested in starting a business similar to theirs and that you admire what they have done. Request to interview them with a few questions for a project you are working on. Since you are a student they'll likely be willing to grant you some time on the phone, or better yet a lunch meeting.

Do your best to leave a good impression and build a relationship with the person you speak with. If they are going to work with you to get this internship, it helps if they like you and trust you.

Find out what their big challenges are:

- If they could wave a magic wand what problem would they solve?
- What are their goals for the next year and how do they plan to achieve them?
- What advantages do their competitors have and how do they plan to outperform them?
- What advantages do they have and how do they plan to leverage those?
- What metrics do they use to measure success?

3 - Design the job and propose it to your internship program.

Once you find an organization that you would like to work and you have identified a problem or a goal that interests you, create a plan for how you will solve it.

Do some research online and see how other businesses of similar size and industry have solved this problem. Most of the challenges businesses face are not unique, and there's likely hundreds if not thousands who have found a solution. Many businesses will publish blog posts on how they solved a particular problem and outline their process for solving it. Use this as a template for your plan.

- What number or metric will you use to measure your success?
- What tools and skills will you use to move this number?
- What goals will you try to achieve?
- How many hours a week will you work on this problem? (I recommend at least 15)
- How long will you work on this? One semester? One year?
- Who will oversee you on this?

This plan needs to demonstrate to the business that you are willing and able to direct yourself and solve your own problems. You want to show them that you will add value to their work and not waste their time.

If they are willing to host your internship then submit your plan to your advisor at your internship program. Work with your advisor through the application process to qualify for school credit and to be eligible for scholarships.

You can download a 90-day project plan to use as a template for your internship plan at kylegray.io/resources

International internships

It's possible to arrange an international internship. But I only recommend this if you have a well-established relationship with the organization you want to work for, and they have a good reputation.

Build trust first

Your success with getting your custom internship approved will hinge on the relationships and trust you build with the business you want to work for and with your internship program. Don't be discouraged if either say "no" at first. A "no" right now is not a "no" forever; learn why you plan was rejected and be prepared for next time.

Consider doing an established internship first to get your feet wet and to prove that you are capable and trustworthy. Do a great job, and keep in touch with your internship advisor. As they get to know you better, they will be more inclined to help you.

In the next chapter we'll discuss in more detail ways you can build skills working within a small business as an apprentice.

Key takeaways

- An internship is a great way to get out of the classroom and into the real world.
- You can create your own custom internship to build exactly the skills you want.
- Find problems that you want to solve in local businesses or organizations and pitch your idea for an internship to them.
- If you don't get approved for a custom internship right away, you can do an internship that has already been arranged with your school to prove that you can handle the responsibility.

Chapter 21

THE APPRENTICESHIP RENAISSANCE

"The goal of apprenticeship is not money, a good position, a title, or a diploma, but rather the transformation of your mind and character." - Robert Greene - Mastery

Before I worked in a startup I had very little understanding of what was important for long term success in my own business.

An apprenticeship changed everything for me. I was able to work in a growing business, be responsible for the main engine of growth for the business (content marketing), and observe how the founders ran the business and planned for its long term-growth. **Taylor Pearson**, author of "**The End of Jobs**," refers to this as "training at altitude."

I had just graduated with my master's degree; my business Conversion Cake was up and running. I had a few clients, $6,000, and a one-way ticket to Asia. It was time to cross the sea and burn the ships-- the only direction was forward.

I was a few months away from leaving when an Australian entrepreneur I had been talking with posted an opening in his startup. He was looking for someone to help him with content marketing. His name was **Dan Norris**, and his startup was called **WP Curve**. He had grown this startup almost entirely by creating interesting content that would attract visitors and nurture them into customers

The deal was that I would work hard for a relatively low salary, and in return he would help me start my own business. I would gain valuable experience working with a thriving startup and build out my own brand and reputation in the process.

I stopped everything when I saw the opening. I wrote him immediately and told him I was already planning on attending a conference that he was going to in Thailand and that I was ready to join his team. Two days before I got on the plane to Asia, I was hired.

I met Dan in Thailand, and started working remotely on his team. I was now in charge of the marketing for a quickly growing startup.

Every day I was challenged to find new ways to draw more attention to our business and get more visits to our blog. I had very little guidance other than the simple goals that were set for me. It was not easy at first, but through hard and focused work I picked up the skills I needed quickly and found new ways to move the business forward. During my first month I struggled to get one blog post out. By the time I left we were producing 10 posts a month with a team of contributors and systems to keep the quality of what we were publishing high.

My year working with WP Curve was a huge leap forward for my abilities and for my personal brand. The skills I learned allowed me to offer up a new service for my business and gave me a bigger platform which attracted new customers and better opportunities.

What is an apprenticeshlp?

Apprenticeships are nothing new. This has been a form of education for thousands of years, where masters of a craft would take on a young apprentice to help them with their work. The apprentice would invest time helping with basic tasks and observe the master in action. Over time the tasks the apprentice was in charge of would become more and more intricate. This was the traditional way to learn crafts like blacksmithing, jeweling, pottery and other professions that require years to master.

Today many small businesses are using this model as well. The founder brings on an apprentice to manage a part of the business. The apprentice learns entrepreneurship skills first-hand in exchange for a small salary with the expectation that what they learn now will pay off in the future. As an apprentice, I also had the option to work remotely, so I could live in a place where my small salary would stretch farther.

What's the difference between an apprenticeship and an internship?

Internships are often with large organizations that need an intern for cheap labor to manage low-priority tasks. The tasks are often well-organized and directed, which makes for a predictable experience. Organizations know what they need from their interns and they have defined the responsibilities that their interns will have.

An apprenticeship is often with a small business. With the small team, apprentices have a larger amount of responsibility and are usually in change of more important tasks. As an apprentice, you'll usually receive less direction and have to figure things out for yourself.

Both of these definitions are perhaps over generalized, and there are many cases that fall somewhere in the middle of this spectrum. But for the sake of explanation we'll keep them simple.
Why would you want to do an apprenticeship?
For an aspiring entrepreneur, the hard work and low wages involved in an apprenticeship may seem like a poor choice. Why would someone who wants to be their own boss postpone their own business in favor of working for someone else?

Here's a few reasons why an apprenticeship is valuable:

- **It gives you a model to see how a small business is run** - If you have not worked in a small business or startup before, it can be difficult to imagine what the day-to-day operations are like and how to strategize for long-term growth. Being able to work in a business that is already growing can give you this context.

- **You'll build relationships with potential advocates and customers** - You're not only going to be working with your team members in an apprenticeship. You'll likely be connecting with customers, partners and other friends of the business. These could be potential customers for your future business, future advocates to help promote your business, or other interesting partnerships.

- **You'll learn faster** - An apprenticeship will make you directly responsible for an important part of a business. Learning the skills to manage that responsibility in a live environment will teach you much faster than a course or a book can. You'll also learn how to apply these skills in a practical way. You'll develop these skills using someone else's money. This means you'll have access to resources that you could probably not afford on your own.

- **It is a good source of business ideas** - Apprenticing for a business will show you its inner workings. It will give you a chance to identify problems that you enjoy solving. If you find a problem that one business is willing to pay to solve, it's likely there are many more businesses who need the same solution. This could be the perfect place to find your next business idea.

- **You'll be able to leverage the business' brand to grow your own** - By associating with a growing business you'll connect your brand with theirs. Playing a key role in a successful and growing brand can lend trust to your own. This will mean more and better opportunities in the future and faster growth for your business.

When to do an apprenticeship

The most obvious time for an apprenticeship is right after you graduate. Immediately following graduation, you probably won't have many commitments and if you have been working on building your own business or personal brand while in school, you should have a good track-record to demonstrate that you have something to offer. This will make you an attractive candidate for apprenticeships.

If possible I would encourage you to do an apprenticeship a year before you graduate. You may be able to arrange your apprenticeship as a custom internship, something we discussed in previous chapters. Even if you can't earn credit for your apprenticeship, the experience you gain from spending a year in the "real world" will completely shift how you view your education.

If you can't arrange for credit, some universities will allow you to take time off between semesters and return to the university without having to reapply or retake classes. This option is something you'll need to discuss with your academic advisor. Even without the credit, working for a business will give you valuable experience and could change what you focus on for the remainder of your education.

The skills that you bring back from an apprenticeship can serve as a source of income, an engine of growth for your business, and as direction for how you can best invest your time at the university.

The main goals of an apprenticeship

Save your mentor time - You're here to take responsibility off of your mentor's plate and free them up to focus on other aspects of the business.

Blaze a trail - You're not only here to learn how to do a job well, but to create detailed processes and documents that can be routinely and predictably executed. This will keep you moving forward and constantly solving new problems and will ensure that the value you add to the business is not lost or wasted when you leave.

Develop a skill - Your apprenticeship should be focused on developing a skill or set of skills that are in demand and that people are willing to pay for.

Build a network - You should leverage your mentor's network and brand to start meeting people and developing your own connections. This will make it easier for you to add value to your apprenticeship. Use every opportunity to collaborate with influencers and other businesses. Try to add at least as much value as you receive in every interaction.

Learn the mechanics of a business - This is an opportunity to examine the nuts and bolts of a business and to get a grasp on the details that are happening behind the scenes.

Common misconceptions about apprenticeships

Many people enter apprenticeships hoping for daily coaching sessions for the entrepreneur they are working for transfer knowledge to them. As an apprentice, it is more likely that you will be responsible for directing your own learning. Entrepreneurs are hiring apprentices not out of kindness of their hearts, but because they need help.

An apprenticeship is not for the faint of heart. Usually you are given a problem or a goal and it is up to you to figure out how to solve it. This can be challenging after coming from an education system that is based on giving specific instructions for a specific outcome. Though it can be challenging, an apprenticeship can give you the skills and perspective you need to succeed in starting a business and thriving in the modern economy.

How to find an apprenticeship

Many entrepreneurs will publish job postings for an apprentice-style position on their businesses' blogs. You'll see opportunities appear on social media as well. The key is to start to plug into the communities where apprentice-ships are common. These are typically small startups with an established online presence.

All of these positions are closed, but here are a few previous examples to give you an idea of what to look for:

https://empireflippers.com/content-marketing-hiring-post/
https://www.amztracker.com/blog/work-with-us/
http://wpcurve.com/were-hiring/

There are also services like **Get Apprenticeship** that email you notifications about new opportunities for free.

How do I start to connect with these communities?

There's a few common traits to businesses in apprentice-friendly communities:

- They value remote work and are location independent - so you see them in places like Chiang Mai, Thailand, Ho Chi Minh City, Vietnam, Barcelona, Spain and more.

- They tend to focus their marketing efforts online and have blogs, pod-casts and youtube channels.

- They rely heavily on technology and outsourcing to keep costs low and to be competitive.

Tips for applying for apprenticeships

When it comes down to sifting through hundreds of applicants you want to do everything possible to stand out.

Research the person who is hiring - Before you apply, it's best to have a good understanding of the person who is hiring and what their needs and interests are. Take some time to look at their social media channels and research what they are posting about. Find their personal blog and read through some of their posts. Use this information to start building a relationship with them.

Lead with "you" not "I" - When you are writing your application, focus on the perspective of the person hiring you, not your own perspective. Instead of stating everything about yourself, i.e. "I have this experience… I have these skills…", frame it in the context of something they want, i.e. "You need someone with this experience to help you with X." This makes it easier for them to visualize how you would fit in with the company and what problems you would solve.

Be a natural fit - Dan Andrews from **Tropical MBA** has been through a few hires of apprentices. When explaining how to get your dream job he empha-sizes how you want to frame yourself as a "natural fit":

"The best way to show that you are enthusiastic about the position is to underscore the things that you are already doing and why those projects and passions lead naturally to something like the position you are applying for. This is critical for me: I don't want to be a "big" opportunity for people. That's a risk. I want to be a "natural" opportunity. Understanding this difference is critical for successful deal-making in general."

Create a video - Many apprenticeship applications request that you create a video to introduce yourself and show your personality.

With all the antics and shock value that we see from videos on Youtube and Facebook these days, it's easy to be tempted to do something that you think will be funny or memorable on these videos. This is usually a bad idea.

Keep things very simple. Sit in front of a camera and talk about yourself and expand on what you wrote in your application. Be confident, smile, and address specific points on the job posting.

If you want to add some flare, do so in a way that reinforces that you are a good fit, not just to get attention. Remember Vincent's video from the personal branding chapter? He reached out to thought leaders and influencers to help him make his video unique and powerful.

Propose your own apprenticeship

Perhaps you have searched and can't find an opening that's right for you. Maybe you have found businesses you would like to work with, but they don't have an apprenticeship opening for you. The concept of an apprenticeship is still unfamiliar to many businesses, so they many not even be aware it's an option.

If you know of a business or an entrepreneur that you would like to learn from, you can propose your own apprenticeship to them. Start by building a relationship with the business using some of the strategies we have looked at in other chapters. Try to get a feel for where the business could use your help. I recommend starting with marketing. Marketing is something every business could use more of, and it is a skill that you can use for your own business in the future. Even if marketing is not your strongest area or what you would want to focus on, it is often the easiest way to get your foot in the door.

Once you identify a problem that you would like to work on, put together a plan to help solve that problem. Do the same research that was outlined in the previous chapter on custom internships.

Once you have the problems identified, it's time to put Ramit Sathi's "**Briefcase Technique**" into action. This sounds simple and obvious, but it is an incredibly powerful way to sell yourself and leave a strong impression:

1. List all the problems you have identified in a single document.
2. Put together a brief plan about you will solve each of them. This plan should be about 2-4 pages. It should look and feel almost like a menu at a restaurant filled with solutions to their problems. Be as detailed as possible about how you will solve the problems and the time frame you expect it would take to solve each one.
3. If possible, schedule an in-person meeting with the owner of the business. If not, do a Skype video call.
4. Pull the document out of your briefcase (yes, go get one even if you only ever use it for this moment) and hand it to them.

If you have found the right problems and given compelling solutions, the business owner should be salivating.

Offer to enact one of the solutions you have planned for free. If you do it well and prove the value of your work, you'll earn a paycheck easily and skip the tedious application processes.

You can download a 90-day project plan to use as a template for your apprenticeship proposal at kylegray.io/resources.

Make your apprenticeship a custom internship

If you have a business that is willing to work with you on an apprenticeship, use this opportunity to get university credit by making it a custom internship. Most apprenticeships are highly challenging and rewarding and should fit in nicely with most university's requirements for a custom internship.

Key Takeaways

- An apprenticeship can dramatically change the direction of your life and change the trajectory of your business through helping you develop competitive skills and valuable relationships.
- Doing an apprenticeship for a year or so before you graduate could be one of the most transformational experiences of your education.
- Remember that your main goal is to save your mentor time and make their life easier. You'll need to be independent and find solutions to problems on your own.
- Remember when applying to focus on the solutions you'll provide for them, not what they will do for you.
- Use the "Briefcase technique" to pitch your own apprenticeship.

Chapter 22

A GUIDE TO DROPPING OUT

Chandler Bolt entered school as a business major with aspirations to learn how to build a business. He grew up wanting to own a business and expected to learn the fundamentals as a business major. Chandler was driven to learn practical skills to get specific results. He was not working to earn a degree, nor did he expect a degree was the "permission" he needed to do what he wanted to do.

But as Chandler started going through classes he was not satisfied with what he was learning. Many of the professors he was learning from were teaching theory and had never started or run a business before. Chandler wanted to learn by doing, not from theoretical discussions or fancy academic vocabulary.

Chandler found an internship that gave him some hands-on experience starting and running six figure businesses. With the confidence and practical experience gained from these internships, Chandler knew he was ready to be done with classrooms and to finally start his own business.

It was not an easy choice. He spoke with his friends and family about it, and nobody agreed that it was a good idea. Except for one friend, a trusted mentor. Even his mentor said it was not something he would recommend for most people, but for Chandler, it seemed like the right move.

This was one of the most difficult decisions Chandler had ever made, but he knew deep down what he wanted to do and he was not going to put it off because of others' expectations of him.

Once he left school, he decided to take a few months to travel through Europe before he dove into building a business. He wrote a short book on productivity and launched it from his laptop while traveling.

The early stages of his business weren't easy. He started developing his business around the book **The Productive Person**. He created courses and other services related to concepts in the book. He was struggling to make progress and was losing money. Some big deals he was counting on fell through and he started to question if leaving school was the right choice. But after her returned from Europe, his book was bringing in a steady 2-3k each month. That income was his lifeline to keep him moving forward and growing his business.

Chandler continued to help others with book launches, and he was constantly getting emails from people asking how he engineered such a successful book launch. Since his current business was struggling, he put an offer out looking for people who would be interested in learning how to launch their first book. This project evolved into **Self-Publishing School**, a program that helps authors write, publish and promote their own books.

The path was not easy, and it was not always clear that dropping out was the right call. But Chandler trusted his instincts and committed to being an entrepreneur.

Dropping out

As you progress with your business, you may find yourself at a crossroads. Your business may be showing a lot of potential. You may have customers coming in quickly. Maybe you are even considering hiring some help. But perhaps your business has grown so big that it is starting to conflict with your studies. You may start of feel constrained by your university rather than enabled by it.

You may be tempted to shed the burdens of your university and focus on growing your business. Maybe you don't feel like what you are learning is valuable, or that you could better invest your tuition money in other places.

Maybe other opportunities have presented themselves. Through the process of making connections to grow your business, sometimes a high-paying job offer surfaces with a startup you admire and they want you to join right away. Though these things are tempting, it's not an easy choice to leave behind school to pursue other things. How can you make this call?

Big decisions and bad information

Dropping out is a topic that is taboo and sensationalized, which makes it very difficult to get objective information. It almost seems like it is required that a successful entrepreneur drops out of college first, or that dropping out should be a badge of honor and recognition in the startup community. Then on the other end there's horror stories of dropouts who live out unhappy lives as a result of their choice.

It is easy to conjure up stories of startup legends like Mark Zuckerberg, and cite their success as reasons why you should drop out as well. We often make the mistake of oversimplifying a complex set of decisions and circumstances to make things easy to understand. What seems like a "happily ever after" tale about how someone dropped out to grow a billion dollar business is often only part of the story.

Though the dropout stories are now commonplace, it can be misleading to think that these success stories happen all the time. Statistically, dropping out hoping to start a million dollar business is not unlike dropping out to prepare for the NBA draft. These aren't great odds to make a bet on.

The millions of students who drop out every year but don't create successful businesses are not likely to become media headlines.

"These are the 34 million Americans over 25 with some college credits but no diploma. Nearly as large as the state of California, this group is 71 percent more likely to be unemployed and four times more likely to default on student loans. Far from being millionaires, they earn 32 percent less than college graduates, on average." The Atlantic

But even this too is sensationalized. This data lumps intrepid student entrepreneurs who want to grow a business with a giant mass of other students who drop out for a myriad of other reasons. It's unfair to consider the intrepid entrepreneurial student in this category. But that's what these statistics are doing, and that distorts the reality of the situation.

Even Bill Gates, a legendary drop out himself, has praised a degree and the skills that come with it.

"College graduates are more likely to find a rewarding job, earn higher income, and even, evidence shows, live healthier lives than if they didn't have degrees. They also bring training and skills into America's workforce, helping our economy grow and stay competitive. That benefits everyone".

It's just too bad that we're not producing more of them."
Bill Gates - Help Wanted: 11 Million College Grads

So with conflicting information on both sides, how can you make a good decision? Dropping out requires that you do a very honest self-assessment and examine your business to make sure this is truly the best path for you. Each situation is unique and only you will be able to recognize the best solution for you.

In this chapter I will provide you with many different tools and perspectives that you can use to make the decision that works for you.

Don't make big decisions based on emotions

Have you ever been so wrapped up in anger that you say things you later regret? Or caught up in a romance with someone that "feels so right" in the moment, but you later realize how poorly they treated you?

Emotions cloud our thinking. They override the logical areas of our brain and make it difficult to make good decisions. The high-stakes choice of dropping out is almost certain to stir up emotions in you and those closest to you.

If you are under 25, remember that your brain has not completely developed. The region known as the "prefrontal cortex" which is largely associated with decision-making has not fully matured.

"Changes occurring between ages 18 and 25 are essentially a continued process of brain development that started during puberty. When you're 18, you're roughly halfway through the entire stage of development. The prefrontal cortex doesn't have nearly the functional capacity at age 18 as it does at 25". Mental Health Daily

That is not to imply that you cannot make a good decision. But it does mean that you are more likely to be influenced by emotion. It is important that you do everything possible to ensure you are clear-minded and give this decision the careful consideration it deserves.

One of the easiest ways to do this is to clear your mind of emotion before making the call to drop out. Whether you are feeling euphoric or enraged, both positive and negative emotions will influence how you perceive your situation.

There are a few ways to separate your decision from your emotions:

- **Schedule time to think** - This is not a choice that should be made on a whim, thought out on your walk between classes, or in the heat of fury after that "nasty professor" frustrates you again. Schedule some time when you can be free of distractions, in a quiet place, and give yourself the space to think this through. You may be surprised by how differently you see the situation after some clear and focused thought.

- **Brain dump in your journal to work through emotions** - If you can't seem to escape the emotions when you are faced with this decision, let yourself dump them out on paper. Focus on what you are feeling and thinking and translate that from thoughts into words. Give in completely to the emotions and let them flow through you into writing. The emotions should start to disappear or diminish. Once they are on paper, you may find your thoughts or emotions to be less logical or useful than they seemed in your head.

- **Talk to a mentor** - If you have developed connections with entrepreneurs, business owners and other thought leaders, share your thoughts about dropping out with them. Give them details about why you feel your university is holding you back and what you want to do once you are out. They won't have the same emotions tied to this decision, and may have a very different perspective to offer.

- **"Hell yes" or no** - Entrepreneur, author, and speaker Derek Sivers has a philosophy: if a decision is not something you would say "hell yes" to, then it is a no. Though this contradicts the "emotion free" decision making I just advised, it is a useful lens to consider. If it is something feels like a 9 out of 10 on your "good ideas" scale then go for it. But even if it is and 8, you think it's a pretty good idea, but you still have some minor reservations, then it's a 1, a simple no.

Beware the dip

Don't be fooled by early success in your business. It is common to experience a surge of growth early in your business' life. Like with working out, learning a language, or any other worthwhile pursuit, you are often rewarded with quick growth in the early stages. But this does not last forever. The easy gains are replaced with tedium, uncertainty, and challenges. This is what Seth Godin calls "**the Dip**".

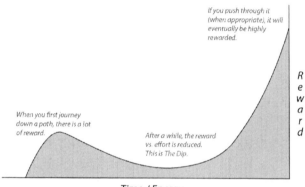

It would be unwise to drop out at the peak of some early success and count on that success to continue only to hit the dip in your business. Though it's impossible to predict what the future holds, you should anticipate large setbacks and be prepared for them. Don't think that you will be the exception to the rule.

That's not to say that the threat of the dip should keep you from taking risks and going all-in on your business. Dropping out to focus on your business to get through the dip may be the way to success. But you must be aware of it. Know that you are committing to the hard road and greater rewards in the future.

The dip in your university career

Like I mentioned earlier, "the Dip" does not just apply to businesses. It applies to almost any skill or project. So it is worth asking yourself if you are going through "the Dip" in your academic career currently. Maybe things are hard at school, and things aren't going to plan. Maybe you did not get the scholarship you were counting on, or you were not approved for the custom internship you wanted for next semester.

It is easy to be frustrated with the "red tape" and setbacks that you'll experience at a university. If you have tried some of the strategies in this book, you are likely to run up against all kinds of barriers. Learning to navigate these barriers is a slow process, and it should not be abandoned at the first sign of resistance.

"... never quit something with great long-term potential just because you can't deal with the stress of the moment". Seth Godin - The Dip

Make sure you drop out into something

Don't leave with the blind hope that something will work out. You should have something promising to drop into.

If you are dropping out to focus on your business, be prepared to give it everything you have. Though you'll free up time and energy by leaving the university, you should be working harder than ever to ensure the success of your business. This is an "all in" bet and you should treat it like that. Don't make this bet until your business is providing some income to support you and is stable enough that you can rely on it.

Don't expect to "wing it" when you drop out. Have a detailed plan and measureable goals that you set out to achieve. You should know exactly how you will spend your extra time and energy.

Maybe you are offered an interesting job that pays well or has potential to become something big. Perhaps the offer is coming from a new startup that shows promise, and you have a chance to get in early and reap the rewards of its success. If this is your first full-time job offer, it can be tempting to abandon your education or your own business.

But make sure you understand the risks. Remember that the billion-dollar exits are rare and the failure rate of startups is high. You may end up working very hard for little in return. Though you'll have the opportunity to learn and grow your network, make sure you're not getting an offer that's too good to be true.

Maybe you have an offer with a more mature business that's not likely to fold. Make sure you are getting more than just a salary. Taking on a high paying job that does not challenge you, allow you to continue growing your skills, or surround you with people who help you will only cause you to stagnate, and may not be worth the sacrifice in the long run.

"I'll do it later"

A common way to rationalize dropping out is by telling yourself that you'll come back and finish your degree later. But studies find students returning to college have a much lower completion rate than first-time students. Students that leave and return again are more likely to become repeat dropouts.

"In the first national effort to benchmark the persistence patterns of non-first-time college students, researchers found that only 33.7 percent of non-first-time

students completed their degree, compared with 54.1 percent of first-time students".

http://www.insidetrack.com/2014/10/27/
national-study-non-first-time-students-shows-disturbing-completion-rates/

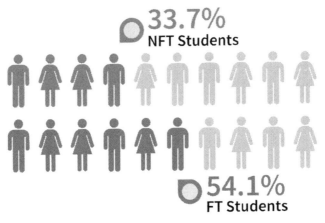

33.7%
NFT Students

54.1%
FT Students

NFT Count 4,581,124

FT = First-time
NFT = Not first-time

This does not necessarily mean it's bad news for the entrepreneurial drop out. Perhaps with a successful business and a valuable skillset, returning to finish your degree won't be necessary for your professional development.

If you are dropping out to pursue a business then your story could be very different from most of the students surveyed here. But the point is not to deceive yourself with a common excuse. "I'll do it later" is probably the most common rationalization that holds people back from doing anything great.

Whether it's quitting their job to travel the world, finally writing that book, getting in shape, or anywhere else you experience "the Dip," the idea of putting it off for later is always looming.

So beware of the toxic philosophy of "I'll do it later." If that is the first argument you list when considering dropping out, you should find better reasons. Don't let this set a precedent for putting off other difficult and rewarding things in your life.

Have a set plan to return:

Roslyn and her business partner Robin from **Made Real** faced the challenge of balancing a growing business and school demands. To keep the business healthy one of them needed to focus on it full-time. They came up with a creative solution that would allow the business to grow without forcing them to completely drop out.
They decided to alternate who would work on the business full-time and who would stay in school each semester. This way, each of them continued to play a vital role in the business and they could also allow themselves to finish their degrees.

It's not always possible to have a strong partnership like Roslyn and Robyn, but you can still borrow their strategy. Instead of completely dropping out, consider taking a semester off to focus on your business.

On your semester off, focus on finding ways to bring on a business partner or team members, to automate time-consuming tasks, or to outsource. One of the best books to help you create systems that allow you to delegate tasks and outsource your work is called **Work the System** by Sam Carpenter. You can download the book for free from his website.

If you are able to hand off some of your workload, you'll be able to return to school without having to sacrifice your business. The practice of delegating tasks will come in handy in the future as well.

Have a source of income

Make sure you are earning enough to support yourself before you unplug from your university. If you drop out to focus on your business, only to end up getting a job to help pay the bills a few months later will leave you torn between your business and other responsibilities.
Using leftover student loans as a way to finance your new business is not only a bad idea, it's illegal. Loan money is not the kind of money you want to become accustomed to relying on either. Remember that your loans will go into repayment mode shortly after you drop out, so factor that cost into your daily expenses.

Many scholarships have conditions that you need to repay them if you drop out, even if you used them years ago. Make sure you understand the terms of any scholarships you have been awarded (or may be awarded in the future) before you make the choice to drop out.

If you believe you have a truly exceptional business idea, consider applying for the **Thiel Fellowship**. This fellowship is designed for students who want to leave university to chart their own course and build something incredible. The award is up to $100,000 for students to drop out and focus on their projects.

Consider what's at stake

You'll leave behind more than just classes when dropping out. There are other things you'll want to be prepared to leave before you make the move.

Motivation

It is important to ask yourself if you have the self-discipline to continue progressing without the well-defined schedule that a university provides. You'll need focus, organization, and grit to keep moving forward with your business.

You need to be working on something that you care about enough to continue learning and growing. Just because classes are out does not mean that your education stops; you'll simply have to direct it yourself. Though it's possible to learn almost anything online, you'll need to have the drive to teach yourself and the wisdom to discern the value of the information you are taking in.

You'll need to stay strong in good times and bad, and there will be plenty of both. Make sure you are ready for the hardships and uncertainty that come with entrepreneurship.

You need to be comfortable enough in yourself and what you are doing that you can take risks in order to grow. Dropping out is a sign that you are open to taking risks, but don't expect things to get easier from there.

You lose access to resources

By now you should have a good idea of the amount of resources available to you at your university. Universities are hotbeds for innovation and collaboration. You'll find that growing relationships outside of the university and without support can be much more difficult. The best and the brightest people you'll want to work with will be scattered across the country and the world, all with their own schedules and priorities. At university you have brilliant minds within walking distance every day, and the commonalities you share as a member of that university make it one of the easiest times to develop relationships.

If your business targets students or young people, then you will be losing one of the best connection points to your customers. Pulling potential partners and customers is as easy as getting some pizzas (and making your university pay for them) and having a meetup or an event focused on a problem you want to learn about solving.

You'll also lose access to university resources to help build your business. This includes resources like computer labs, alumni networks, or even the "title of student" like we discussed in previous chapters. Many universities also have advanced equipment like 3D printers, or other technology that might be difficult to find or expensive to use off campus. Do some thorough research and make sure you don't leave anything behind that you might regret not having access to later.

Resources for student entrepreneurs

Though the Thiel Fund is an enticing offer to aspiring entrepreneurs who are considering dropping out, there's a growing number of resources specifically for student entrepreneurs:

The **Dorm Room Fund** provides resources for student-run companies.

The **Rough Draft** foundation also provides funding and resources for student-run businesses in the Boston area.

Even if your university does not offer resources specific to student entrepreneurs, many states offer state-wide business plan competitions with large cash prizes, exposure for the competitors, and mentoring from entrepreneurs to help develop student businesses. **The Utah Entrepreneur Challenge** offers five-figure cash prizes and is open to any student in the state.

Business plan competitions aren't limited to the United States either. You can find national student business plan competitions in many countries across the world. **Studentcompetitions.com** has an extensive list of competitions and resources.

Who is watching your back?

A trend amongst the successful dropouts is that they had a strong network and set of skills. You'll want to be sure you have a support system in place for the transition out of school in case you hit any unexpected setbacks.

It's worth having a discussion with your family about dropping out. It will likely be a difficult conversation, but a necessary one. Even if they aren't supportive of your decision, it is better to discuss it with them now rather than surprise them with the news that you have left school once it is too late.

You should also have a strong professional network to call on once you drop out. Having strong relationships with people in your industry will help guide you through this transition and send opportunities your way.

Key Takeaways

- Dropping out will be one of the most important decisions of your life (up to this point). Remember that your situation is completely unique, so don't be overly enticed by the stories of other's successes or by dismal statistics of failures.
- Make sure you are dropping into something; have a plan before you leave.
- Have a source of income established and a network to support you if you choose to drop out.

- Be sure you are well-aware of what you are giving up when dropping out.
- Beware of "the Dip" in your business, don't count on early successes to continue.
- With some careful consideration, and an honest self-examination, you'll be able to make the right choice for you and your business.

Chapter 23

THE CROSSROADS

Here you are, at the closing chapter of this book.

But your story is just beginning.

You've come to a crossroads; it's time to make a choice. You can choose to follow the same path as everyone else, and get mediocre results. Or you can choose to take control of your education and use it to build something that you are proud of and live life on your own terms.

You have what it takes; by making it this far in the book you have already proven it. You've invested your time and money to improve yourself. You've opened your mind to new ideas and you have followed your curiosity and passion. Stay connected with this energy and you'll see great results in your college career and throughout your life.

Many of the ideas in this book are concepts that can serve you far beyond your time at university. Your time spent developing these skills will pay off in ways that you can't imagine or anticipate at this point. So get excited and take courageous action!

Not everyone will understand your newfound goals or aspirations. Like my friends and family did with me, they may think you are crazy, selfish or arrogant. Don't let them discourage you.

Now that you know these strategies, a whole new world of opportunity has opened up to you. But you have to choose to use them and find ways to make them work for you.

Remember not to try too many of these ideas at once and don't be discouraged if they don't work for you right away. Also, don't be discouraged if you don't have the whole plan figured out yet. It make seem like I knew exactly what I was doing in the stories I shared with you. But it was quite the opposite, I often felt like I was swinging at a piñata in a dark room. I figured it out as a went along, and so will you.

You'll find some that work well for you and your goals. Focus on those instead of trying to achieve everything. I encourage you to revisit the different chapters in this book at times when they are most relevant and useful to you. Combine the strategies that work for you to compound your results.

I wish you the best on this incredible journey, and I hope you share your story with me. I would love to hear about your successes, failures, and all the brilliant ways you make these ideas work for you. You can find me at kylegray.io.

Cheers!

THANKS FOR READING MY BOOK!

I appreciate all of your feedback and love hearing what you have to say.

I need your input to make the next version of this book even better.

Please leave me a helpful review on amazon letting me know what you think of the book.

Thanks so much!!!

Kyle Gray

ACKNOWLEDGEMENTS

Maxine Marshall - Thanks for being such a great team member back in the study abroad office and in bringing out the best in the book.

Elisa Doucette - Thanks for working with me in the early stages of this idea and encouraging me to create something amazing.

Dan Norris - Thank you for giving me a chance to work with you on WP Curve and helping me build the skills and the network that made this book possible.

Scott Paul - Thank you for giving me my very first opportunity to test my skills with Armor Active and for being a great mentor and inspiration to me.

Russ McBride - Thank you for being a great leader in the Foundry and giving me the opportunity to teach a cohort as well.

Chandler Bolt - Thank you for inspiring me to take action on this book and for creating Self-Publishing school. The absolute best resource for new authors out there.

Vincent Nguyen - Thanks for letting me use your story and for being so generous with your knowledge and time.

Mark Manson - Thank you for your constant inspiration with your writing, and for being a friend, reference and mentor since your talk in Utah.

Rob Wuebker - Thank you for believing in me and empowering me to take the first step toward achieving my dreams of starting a business that would allow me to travel. Thank you for being willing to meet with me on an individual basis and guide me through the early stages of by business. And of course for creating the Foundry and the documents that helped transform students into CEOs.

Jay Barney - Thank you for seeing my potential and giving me the chance to teach at the Foundry and help others achieve their dreams.

Cassidy Knight - Thank you for being a friend and inspiration. It's been incredible seeing where life has taken us since that first day of the Foundry.

Kate Galliett - Thank you for supporting me and encouraging me during the creation of this book. Thank you for teaching me how to take better care of myself and inspiring me to push myself forward.
Justin Cooke - Thank you for always being willing to chat with me, share ideas and introduce me to new people. Every conversation we have had has lead to new breakthroughs in my business and my life.

There are countless more people who have been influences and inspirations in my life. I cannot thank you enough.

39548549R00131

Made in the USA
San Bernardino, CA
28 September 2016